NEW GRAPHIC DESIGN
CORPORATE &
INSTITUTIONAL GRAPHICS

LINKS

Edition 2012

Author: Dimitris Kottas
Graphic design & production: Cuboctaedro
Collaborator: Oriol Vallés
Text: Contributed by the architects, edited by Naomi Ferguson

© LinksBooks
Jonqueres, 10, 1-5
08003 Barcelona, Spain
Tel.: +34-93-301-21-99
Fax: +34-93-301-00-21
info@linksbooks.net
www.linksbooks.net

NEW GRAPHIC DESIGN
CORPORATE & INSTITUTIONAL GRAPHICS

LINKS

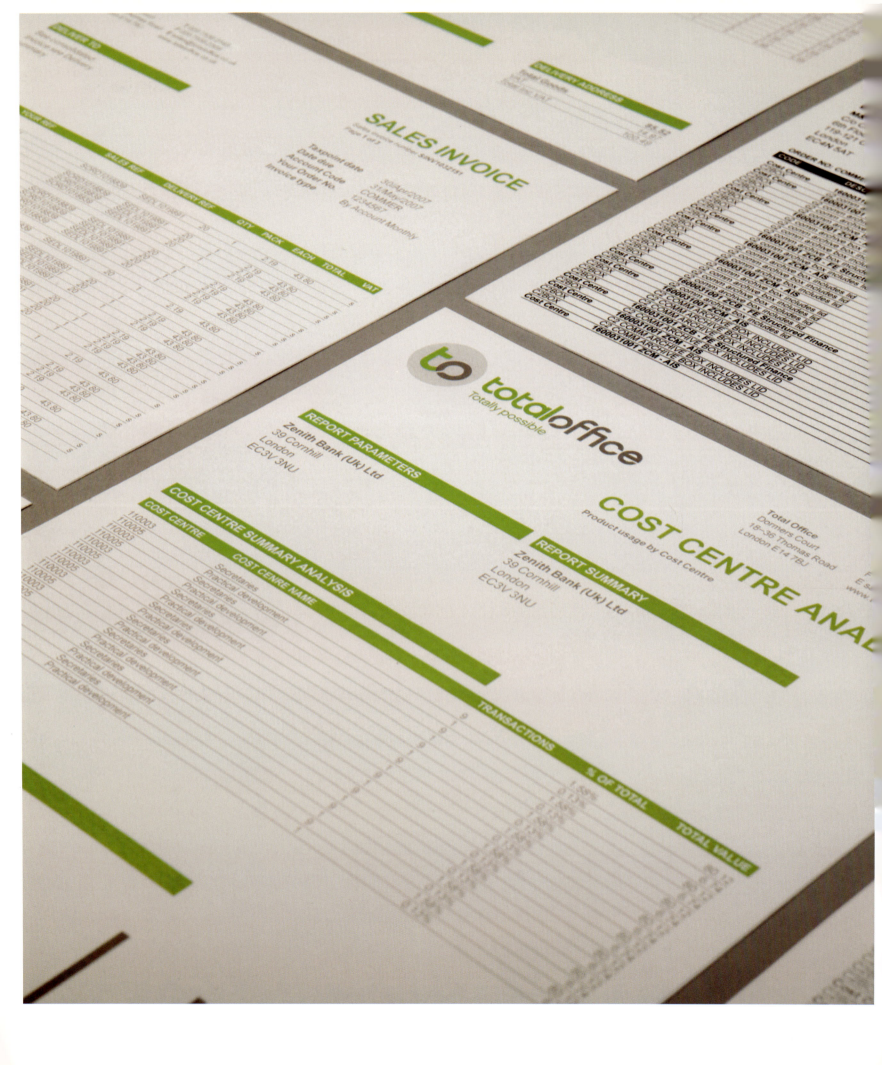

Contents

$2,000,000 —

$1,500,000 —

$1,000,000 —

$500,000 —

$0 —

	Activist-Led Grants	Donor Advised Grants
2003	$311,469	$17,500
2004	$304,050	$21,500
2005	$380,000	$91,000
2006	$368,335	$656,960
2007	$463,840	$144,950
2008	$504,450	$1,170,041
2009	$517,277	$1,330,988

INCOME

Individual Donors
$1,960,220
31%

Fees and Investments
$222,590
4%

Foundation Partners
$175,000
3%

Donor Advised
Partners *
$3,899,270
62%

EXPENSES

...ts and Programs
$1,105,589
37%

...d General
$186,640
6%

...ment
...07

*During the year ended
30, 2008, North Star Fu
entered into an agreemer
with a donor advised part
who was interested in mak
large grants in the South
Bronx. This three-year partnership brought significant
resources to a marginalized
area of New York City. During
the year ended June 30, 2010,
the New York State Public
Service Commission selected
North Star Fund as Greening
Projects Administrator to develop a grantmaking program
that will result in nearly $7.9
million in grants to green the
infrastructure of neighbor-
hoods in Western Queens.

Projects for corporations and institutions are among the most common commissions for a graphic designer. Corporate and institutional clients are plentiful and tend to develop long relationships with one design office, commissioning a great number of projects over a long time span. This enables designers to create a graphic system with various applications that will evolve over time. While not necessarily among the most innovative, corporate projects are technically demanding and require the highest standards of design and production.

Corporate identity graphics have been the mainstay of graphic designers for more than 100 years. From the complete design of AEG's visual presence by Peter Behrens at the beginning of the 20th century to the work of the Swiss Modernists and seminal designers such as Paul Rand and Ivan Chermayeff, projects of this type have defined the history of graphic design.

This long history is a heavy load for contemporary designers, who have to work within fixed frameworks and conventions, while at the same time providing original designs that stand out against the work of their competitors. The rise of the internet and of electronic communications in general has increased the demands on designers, who now have to produce work that is transferable over a wider than ever range of media and adapted to the new contexts.

This book features a selection projects that display both technical excellence and formal innovation. The projects are of all sizes, from business card commissions to complete identity development projects comprising mark, lettering and collateral design together with brand guidelines and white papers to guide the evolvement of the brand identity over time. The works featured do not prescribe to any stylistic preferences other than quality and originality, reflecting our desire to offer an inclusive selection in which the full range of contemporary graphic design tendencies are represented. This volume constitutes an invaluable source of ideas and inspiration for all graphic designers and anyone interested in the field.

B&R

B&R is a legal assessment and services firm formed from the alliance of two previously independent agencies. Anagrama was commissioned to design the new firm's communication material to align the brand with other international legal entities and with a view to long term continuous growth.

The material expresses the identity of the firm in the present and reflects the future that it is working towards.

Pladis

Pladis is a Mexican firm that provides integrated architectural design and construction services.
Anagrama designed the firm's brand identity, and communications materials to reflect their work philosophy and architectural profile.

The designers found the essence of Pladis to be order and structure, manifest as much in their internal operations as in their design work. They identity they developed for the firm is based on Josef Müller-Brockman's grid systems.

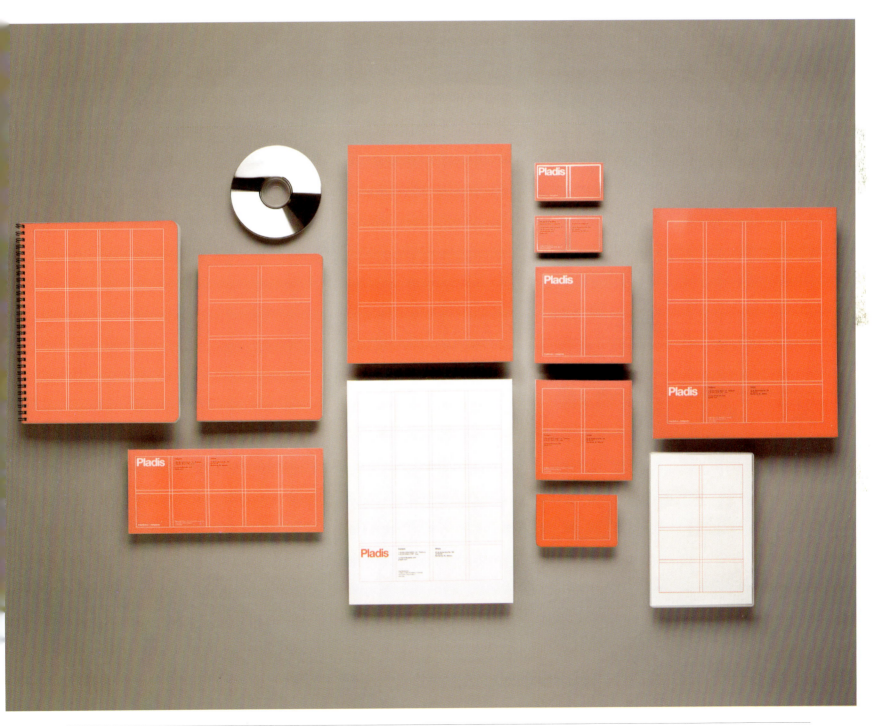

Micheline

Micheline is a printing boutique that specializes in pieces for social events and general stationery. Founded in the mid '70s, Micheline's success derived from offering both design and high-end printing services under the same roof. However as time went by, they realized the potential of appealing to a younger crowd, so the boutique contacted Anagrama to redesign the brand identity and store to reflect uniqueness, elegance, and above all, modernity.

Anagrama designed a monogram that would be easy to reproduce on all of their printed pieces and that would work as a signature for their workshop. With the help of collaborators such as German Dehesa and Roberto Treviño, Anagrama redesigned the store interior, taking inspiration from 'seventies print-shops. The neutral color palette focuses attention on the shelves holding colourful printing catalogues, while emphasizing the brand's presence.

Thanks to Anagrama's branding strategy, Micheline is now a boutique that welcomes all generations, making them feel comfortable and in their own environment.

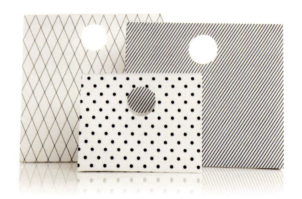

Maria Vogel

Maria Vogel is one of Latin America's foremost up-and-coming fashion designers. When she decided to face the challenging move into high-end markets — a move in which she would come up against strong international competition and a very demanding clientele — she approached Anagrama to design her brand identity.

Anagrama developed a sober, forceful brand identity that conveyed Maria's vision without competing with her imposing designs.

Basing their design on the first Modernist geometric typefaces, Anagrama developed the "Vogel Display" typeface with acute angles that give it a distinctive personality.

The design expresses a solid brand that shows maturity, sobriety and attitude in one of the most selective markets, placing it as a serious competitor to the top fashion houses around the world.

Theurel & Thomas

Theurel & Thomas is the first pâtisserie in Mexico to specialize in French *macarons*, the most popular of the French pastries.

For this project it was very important to create an imposing brand that would emphasize the unique value, elegance and detail of this delicacy.

White was used as the primary vehicle for the design so that all attention would be directed to the colourful pastries. Two lines in in cyan and magenta, a subtle reference to the French flag, inject a vanguardist touch. The typeface is Didot (created by Firmin and Pierre Didot), a French typography infused with sophistication.

En su forma más pura, el macaron francés es una
confección de alta repostería compuesta
por harina de almendra y azúcar.
En su centro atesora un relleno de sofisticados sabores

Theurel & Thomas

NO.350 | L.17

LUNES A SÁBADO
10:00 AM - 8:00 PM

THEUREL & THOMAS

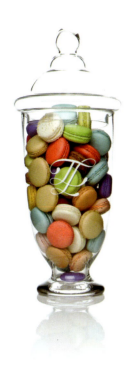

Solberg & Hansen

Solberg & Hansen, one of the best and oldest coffee houses in Norway, established in 1879, has always strived to be the best in the market and offer the finest coffee available. The practice of reading the future in coffee grounds became a central concept in this rebranding project, the designers developing a graphic pattern from the symbols that soothsayers look for in this mysterious process.

Anti had been commissioned to add value to the brand identity and make the logo more sleek. The new brand identity, logo and signature symbol in combination with the typography and information about the coffee helps the brand step up its position in the market. The fresh blue colour and the careful and well thought-out design of this new image sets the brand apart from its competitors.

Chocolate Research Facility

Consider it a world's first: designer chocolate bars offered in 100 different flavours in a concept boutique that's part shop, part laboratory and part art gallery. Focused entirely on chocolate, the brand pays tribute to this divine treat with a myriad of tastes and packaging designs that do more than excite the tastebuds — it's clear that they are serious about elevating the art of chocolate appreciation. From the clinically hip interiors of the boutique to the artful manner of designing, storing and exhibiting the chocolate bars, even to the LED numbers at the storefront, every element expresses the brand philosophy of research, respect and reverence.

Creative Director: Chris Lee
Designer: Yong
Photographer: Lumina Photography
Interior Designer: Cherin Tan

Asylum

TripleOne Somerset

TripleOne Somerset is a new mall dedicated to smart, worldly living. Emphasizing quality and design, its merchandise mix reflects a progressive and international perspective. To visually interpret the diversity of this new retail destination, the brand identity was designed using a cornucopia of colours to convey its promise of providing new shades of shopping experiences. To further differentiate the mall, the designers infused the logo with an element of surprise by making the numeric components of its address appear as if they are popping out of a Jack-in-the-box filled with exciting discoveries.

Creative Director: Chris Lee
Designer: Yong
Photographer: Shooting Gallery

GREEN QUAINT HOT SPOT

Surrounded by greenery, TripleOne Somerset is conveniently located beside Somerset MRT station and within walking distance from the Orchard Road shopping belt. It is bordered by Somerset Road, Grange Road and Devonshire Road, and has long been a landmark for those living in the area as well as the affluent River Valley neighbourhood down the road. Its easy access and ample parking facilities provide a good respite from the crowds at the many undifferentiated malls nearby.

The Somerset area is primed for greater prominence with the development of *SCAPE (a multifaceted recreational space for youth), Discovery Walk (a pedestrian mall lined with shops and cafés over the Stamford Canal) and the area surrounding Somerset MRT. TripleOne Somerset will be a major player in this much-anticipated makeover that will transform Orchard Road.

Fruita Blanch

This corporate identity for the Fruita Blanch family farming company was designed to communicate with the urban consumers that make up the principle clientele of the fruit growers who sell their produce online direct to the consumer. Atipus designed a custom typography for the logo that is friendly and modern.

The graphic system is based on browns and greens to convey closeness to the land, and colours representing the 3 fruits that the company grows (apples, pears and nectarines).

www.fruitablanch.com

POMA PERA NECTARINA

Brogen Averill

The Department Store

Branding for The Department Store, Auckland's
ultimate boutique shopping experience.
Silver award winner at the New Zealand Best
Design Awards.
Judged best new retail shopping experience
worldwide by Monocle Magazine.

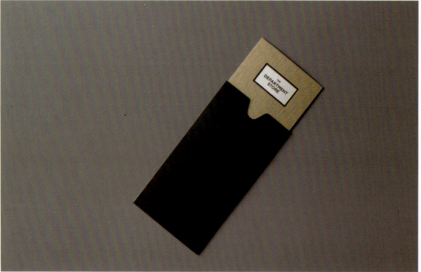

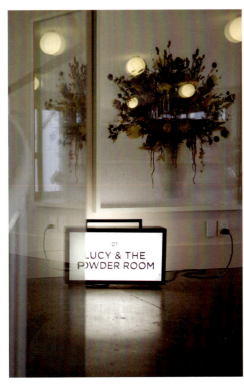

01
LUCY & THE
POWDER ROOM

GF
KAREN
WALKER

GF
SIMON JAMES
DESIGN

02
STEPHEN
MARR

THE
DEPARTMENT
STORE

Brogen Averill

The Department Store Newspaper

The Department Store Newspaper. Bronze
award winner at the New Zealand Best Design
Awards.

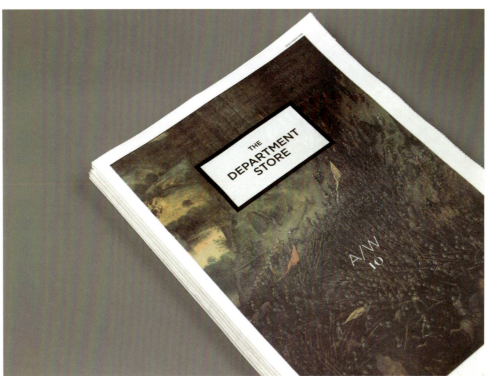

ROUGH DIAMONDS BY DEREK KETTELA

Stylist: Michelle Cameron
Models: Dani at Muse and Anastasia at Muse
Hair by Shin Arima for Stephen Marr using Kevin Murphy
from Stephen Marr
Makeup by Valery Gherman for Marr Lab using Becca
Cosmetics from the Marr lab

SHOT 07
Paisley dress: Opening Ceremony
Distressed jacket: Ksubi

SHOT 08
Blouse: Karen Walker
Cropped jacket and jeans: Ksubi

SHOT 04
White Blouse with puff sleeves
Karen Walker

SHOT 09

Anastasia wears denim jacket with lace sleeves by Stolen Girl

Brogen Averill

Debbie Does

Identity for Debbie 'XXX' – Specialist in strategic communication, corporate communication, human resources and investor relations. Stationery printed using black foil and spot UV over-gloss.

Devonshire Homes - Ashleigh Park

Brand identity and promotional brochure for Devonshire Homes' development, Ashleigh Park. In the absence of actual photography of the development the purpose of the promotional material was to be aspirational and create a strong sense of place. The naming of the development was inspired by it's highly desirable woodland location and each house type is named after a different type of tree. The reverse of each insert features photography of the respective tree leaves. A vivid lime green translucent fly sheet is also incorporated to add a tactile quality and create the effect of sun shining through tree leaves.

Designers: Blair Thomson, Tish England
Photography: Jo Thomson

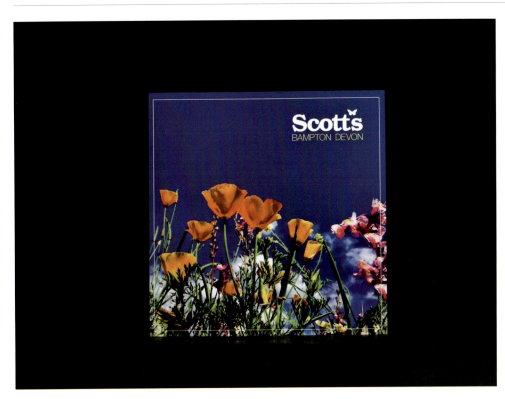

Brand identity and promotional material for Devonshire Homes' development – Scott's. The brochure cover features bright photography of wild flowers to evoke a sense of the rural, countryside location of the development. The wild flower theme is carried throughout the materials, each house type is named after a different wild flower. The vivid colour palette was taken from the cover image.

Designers: Blair Thomson, Tish England
Photography: Jo Thomson

Devonshire Homes - Old Mill Court

Brand identity and promotional material for Devonshire Homes' development – Old Mill Court. The brochure cover features a spot UV varnished large version of the mill-inspired brand identity. The logo is also used as a bold graphic device throughout the brochure. A contemporary take on a traditional setting.

Designers: Gary Meadowcroft
Art Direction: Blair Thomson
Photography: Jo Thomson

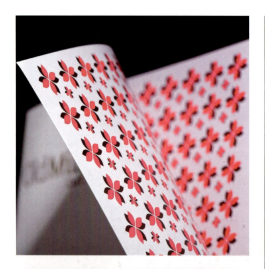

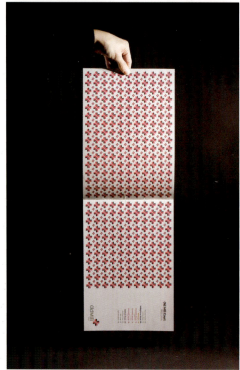

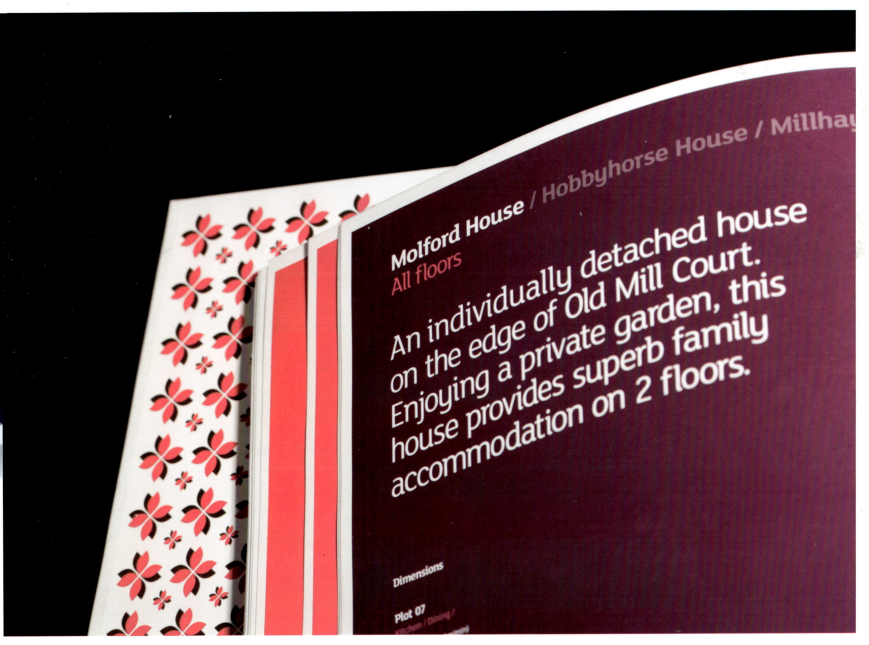

Molford House
All floors

An individually detached house on the edge of Old Mill Court. Enjoying a private garden, this house provides superb family accommodation on 2 floors.

Dimensions

Plot 07
Kitchen / Dining /

Devonshire Homes - Oystercatcher Court

Brand identity and promotional material for Devonshire Homes development 'Oystercatcher Court'. The promotional materials follow a strong coastal theme to capture the highly desirable estuary location of the development. The reverse of each house-type insert features abstract photography of seaside objects and textures. A neutral colour palette together with a bright orange accent comes directly from the colours of an Oystercatcher bird. All materials are uncoated and recycled, to create a highly tactile quality.

Designers: Gary Meadowcroft, Claire Gregory
Art Direction: Blair Thomson
Photography: Jo Thomson

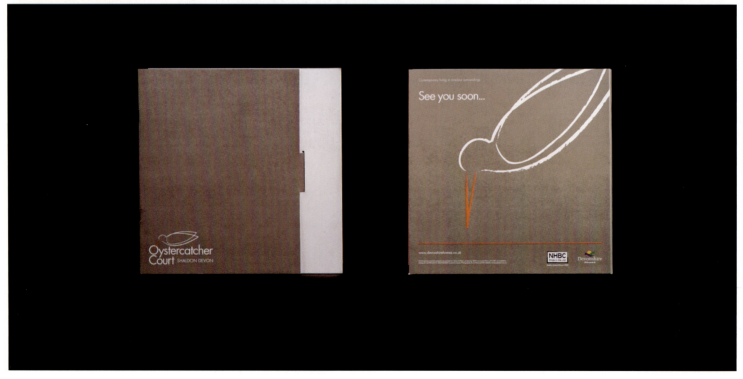

Oystercatcher Court SHALDON DEVON

Val Spicer

Rebranding project for UK based floral foam manufacturer, Val Spicer. The brand identity incorporates a series of flower icons, each created using different formations on the same base shape. This approach is reminiscent of Val Spicer's actual product (floral foam) – the same base foam shape can be used by florists to create many unique floral displays.

The bold, confident brand identity successfully communicates the contemporary design-led approach of the company. The contrasting black and pink creates a strong brand image which reinforces the objectives and positioning of the company and successfully differentiates from their competitors. The identity is memorable, distinctive and easily recognisable.

Designers: Blair Thomson, Tish England
Copywriter: Paul Warren
Photography: Jo Thomson

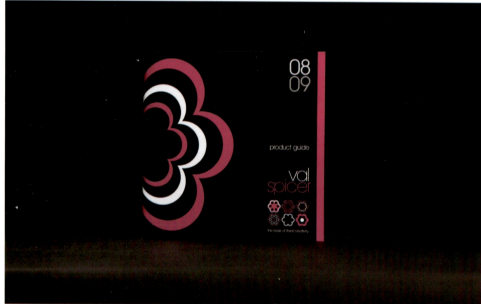

Believe in

Amanda Marsden

Amanda Marsden required a full re-brand after securing the exclusive 'Aveda lifestyle salon & spa' status.

Believe in created a customised typeface to form the contemporary, minimalist 'amanda marsden' wordmark. An abbreviated 'am:' version was developed, which represents the client's initials and also reads as the word 'am', this is used in conjunction with adjectives which reinforce and enhance the brand experience (am: beautiful, relaxed etc.).

Aveda's mission is to strive to set an example in environmental leadership and responsibility. This ethos is reflected in the selected colour palette and materials used, pushing sustainability to the extreme.

Research in Practice for Adults

This brand identity was developed with a colour coded system to represent the six strands of the client's work (learning events, publications, network exchange, Change Projects, website resources and collaborative working). The colours are used independently when referring to a specific activity or used together to create the ripfa spectrum when representing the organisation as a whole. A bold typographic and abstract graphic approach has been adopted throughout the materials.

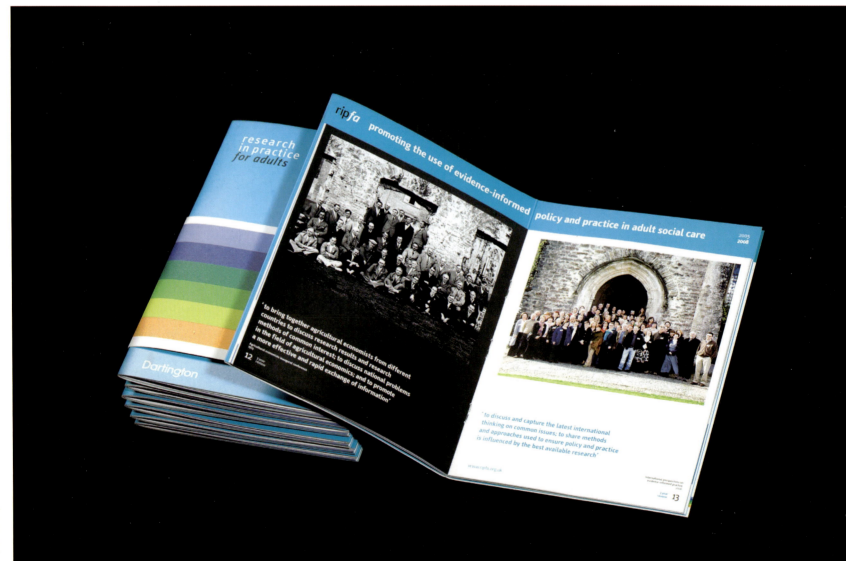

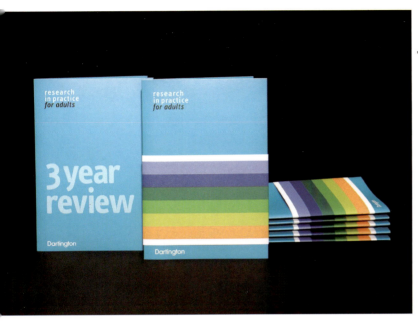

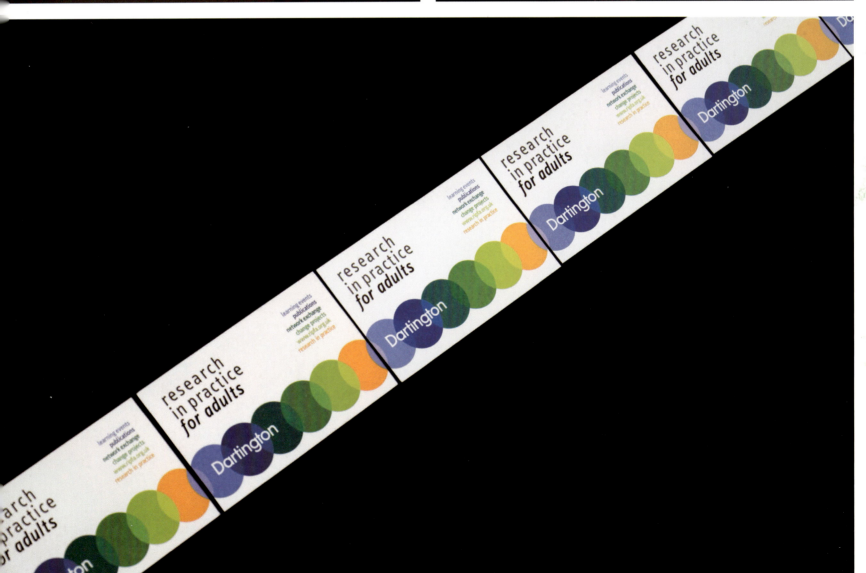

Büro North

Agnes

A new and exclusive development by Periphery Projects with renowned architects Jackson Clements Burrows demanded a highly crafted and bespoke brand identity. The new 4 residence development taking shape in East Melbourne takes architectural cues from the surrounding heritage façades in its unique iron screening, so likewise the brand identity takes classic ornamentation and twists it to create a bold and modern brand mark.

The brochure features an intriguing laser cut pattern referencing the façade's screens and the surrounding Victorian lacework. Inside, the wide format pages are broken up by ethereal photography printed on translucent interleaves.

Team: Soren Luckins, Shane Loorham
Photography: Shane Loorham

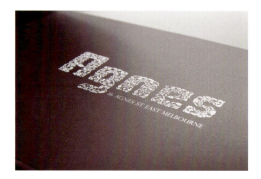

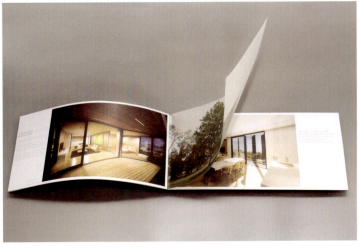

Chris Clarke

Claire Lawson

Design and lettering for Claire Lowson: "claire-lowson - Communications, Creative and Brand Consultant". Comp slips finished on 130 g Pistachio Colourplan. Business Cards finished on 700g Ebony / Pistachio Colourplan.

Chen Design Associates

WebAppFactory

Etched metal, kraft papers and individualized labels were used to create a memorable, flexible identity and business papers system for this web applications developer.

Creative Director: Joshua C. Chen
Designer: Max Spector

Invented brand name and logotype for a metal arts fabrication company specializing in custom made metal fabrication art. As the name and logo suggests, beauty occurs over time beginning with the initial genesis of concept, the continued combination of competing material and shape to final exaltation of form and function.

Art Director: David Conover
Designer: Josh Higgins

StudioConover

Eldorado Stone

StudioConover has been strategizing and creating printed and online communication design for Eldorado Stone since 1995. A co-ordinated effort with their marketing, sales and management departments has conceived websites, online marketing campaigns, printed collateral, direct mail, tradeshow design, packaging, advertising and more.

Art Director: David Conover
Designers: Nate Yates and Andrew Salituri
Copywriters: Michael Fraser and David Conover

HELDER Centre for mental health, self realisation and meditation

'Helder' which means 'clear' in Dutch is a centre for mental health (psychiatric), self realisation and meditation. They also offer training programs and lectures. Each triangle combination creates a unique symmetrical diamond character and refers to the idea of polishing a rough diamond to uncover its inherent pure form. Together with a specially designed geometric monospaced typeface, this motif forms the basis of this identity. All these geometric elements are also present in the Yantra symbol. When combined with textual messages, parts of these 'diamonds' form a frame around quotes from gurus as well as from movie characters and comedians to bring a light hearted humour to the material. A difficult subject treated with a light touch.

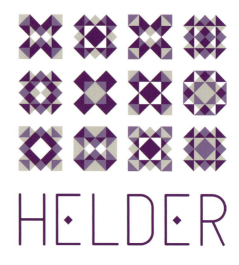

ALWAYS LOOK ON THE BRIGHT SIDE OF LIFE.

MONTHY PYTHON

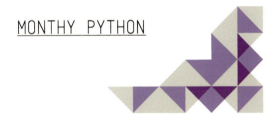

IK BEN NIET LABIEL, IK BEN EMOTIONEEL FLEXIBEL.

THEO MAASSEN

DO OR DO NOT, THERE IS NO TRY.

YODA, STAR WARS V

WEES WAT JE BENT. KOPIEER NIET. VOLG NIEMAND.

MAITREYA

NPT - New Prevention Technologies

New Prevention Technologies (NPT) is a division of the health advocacy group Global Network of People Living with HIV. NPT supports research and development of any health related technology, drug resistance and testing for people living with HIV. Each technology has its own abstract visual clue: vaccines are short vertical lines; microbicides are diagonal dashes; pre-exposure prophylaxis are two horizontal rows of dots; and so on. The booklet (prevention report) shows the visual clues of the technologies that each chapter references into a symbol that looks like a cell under a microscope. The booklet's cover features all the technologies 'mashed' into one circle. The booklet was produced for distribution among HIV/ AIDS policy makers.

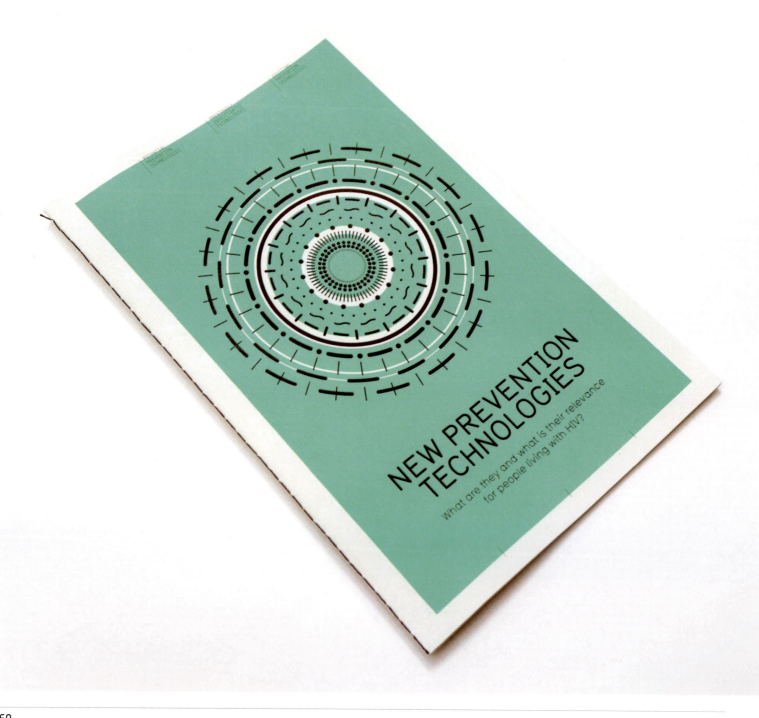

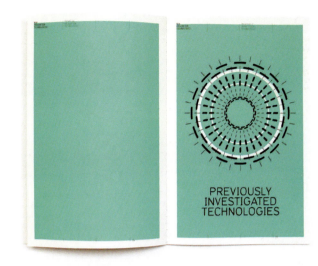

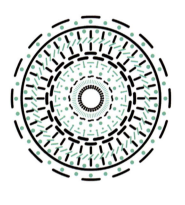

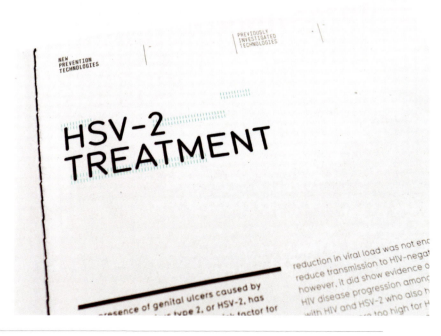

The Canoe Group

When the designers at Counterform met the Canoe Group, and learnt they did not in fact sell canoes, they realised that they were in for a challenge. The shared consulting practice, comprised of four individuals with diverse and specialized backgrounds, needed an identity and a way to re-introduce itself to new and existing contacts.

Counterform took full advantage of the consultancy's name (and their personal appearance) and provided them with an unforgettable way to break the ice at their next meeting.

Whimsical Candy

Whimsical Candy was founded by someone who at age 3 packed her bag and tried to move into a candy store. Not an entirely bad idea. Now a trained pastry chef, she makes small batch sweets that blend a grown-up taste for quality with the fun and classic flavors of childhood candy.

Counterform was called in early for business strategy consulting, naming, and to develop brand identity and packaging. With great salesmanship they were also able to negotiate a small role in product tasting. After several days spent staring at the delicious little round candies, the designers realised that they were staring back at them.

Whimsical
ARTISANAL CANDY THAT'S PURE FUN

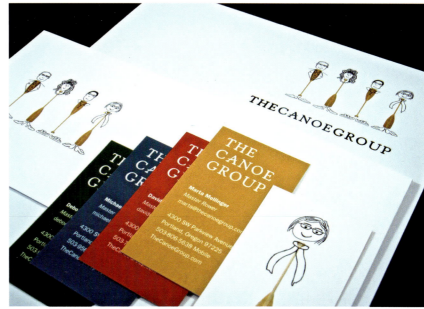

Dalston Creative

Castra

Castra is a 30+ people IT consultancy based in Gothenburg (Sweden).They are now expanding and branching out in Stockholm, and that was the reason for the new brand refresh. Dalston Creative worked with communication agency The Study on the strategy and planning for this project.

The goal was to create a strong brand identity with a set of new marketing initiatives to be in place for 2011. The Study worked out a strong strategy plan with a new deliverable offer to make Castra stand out. This new offer needed an equally special identity to present the new brand initiative, and that's were Dalston Creative came in.

They split the brand into two areas: the "main brand" and a "campaign brand" which received slightly different treatment. A logotype packed with positivity and strong values was developed to accompany a set of marks (icons) that would carry the new brand offer and values within campaigns and marketing.

Dalston Creative created a range of deliverables including logotypes and symbols/marks, all templates (word, ppt etc.) and a full 56 page brand guide covering everything from logotypes, colours, stationary and image usage.

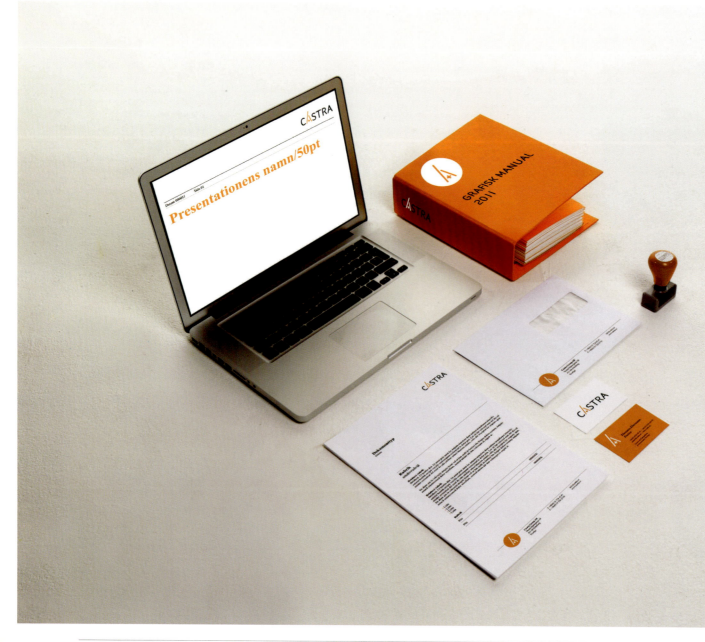

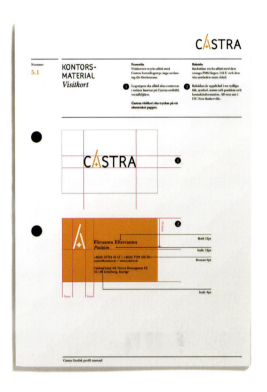

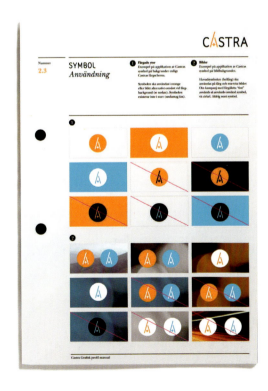

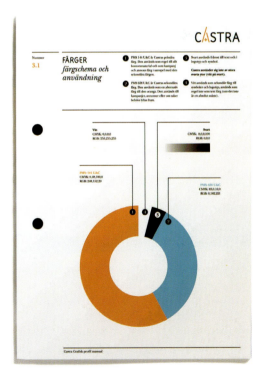

Detail

CRANN

CRANN is a centre for Science and Engineering Technology based in a unique building in Trinity College, Dublin, that provides advanced nanoscience laboratories and facilities. Detail developed their branding and communications programme and have worked on their strategic communications to industry partners, government and business.

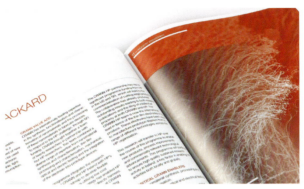

Detail

You Are In

Detail worked with The School of Art, Design &
Printing at the Dublin Institute of Technology
to brand their induction day communications
material for new undergraduates. Helping them
get to know each other, understand the college
and its facilities and find their way around the
campus were the requirements of this simple,
low budget campaign.

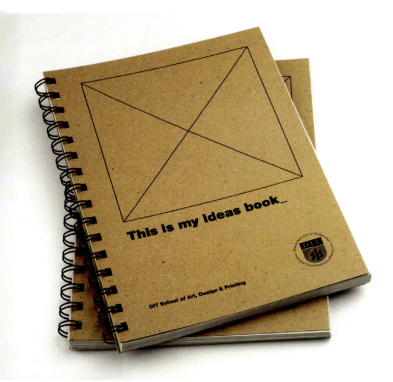

Elixir Design

California Academy Of Sciences

Since 1853, the California Academy of Sciences has been dedicated to exploring, explaining, and protecting the natural world. Prompted by damage sustained in the Loma Prieta earthquake of 1989, the Academy selected Pritzker Prize-winning architect Renzo Piano to redesign the facility. Construction began in 2005 on the largest cultural renovation project in San Francisco's history, uniting the planetarium, aquarium, and natural history museum under one "living roof." To herald the reopening on September 27, 2008 in Golden Gate Park, the Academy planned an opening gala — The Big Bang — to benefit education programs, and two dinners to honor the leaders and philanthropists whose vision and generosity had made the new building a reality. Elixir's designs for the three events reinforced the new Academy brand and invited recipients to come closer, asking "How did we get here? How can we stay?"

Invitations were printed with soy inks on 100% recyclable materials, including Nori seaweed, 100% recycled chipboard, reused pages from Scientific American magazines, and aluminium foil.

Designers: Aine Coughlan, Syd Buffman
Creative Director: Jennifer Jerde

EARTH
250,000 MILES AWAY

SAN FRANCISCO
200 MILES AWAY

THE ACADEMY
1000 FT AWAY

RSVP

CALIFORNIA ACADEMY OF SCIENCES
GOLDEN GATE PARK
55 MUSIC CONCOURSE DRIVE
SAN FRANCISCO, CA 94118

TROPICAL FISH
2 FEET AWAY

CHAMPAGNE
10MM

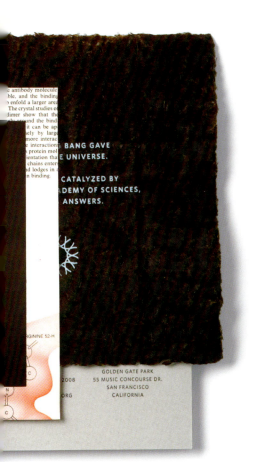

BANG GAVE
E UNIVERSE.

CATALYZED BY
ADEMY OF SCIENCES,
ANSWERS.

GOLDEN GATE PARK
55 MUSIC CONCOURSE DR.
SAN FRANCISCO
CALIFORNIA

Naturopathica

Naturopathica — founded in 1995 and based in East Hampton, New York — reached out to Elixir to rebrand itself with a relaunch of its skin and beauty products. At that time, the line was carried by select high profile spas around the country and sold direct online. Naturopathica enjoyed a small loyal following but was frustrated by a fiercely competitive marketplace brimming with false claims. Barbara Close, Founder and CEO, knew the brand was flying under the radar and suspected that the

packaging's home-grown look and misperceptions about the performance of botanical skin care were factors that needed to be addressed. As part of their North Star process, Elixir Design conducted 1-on-1 interviews with current & prospective customers and spa partners to help Naturopathica understand how their brand was perceived. The findings illuminated the gap between current perceptions and desired positioning, inspiring the company to undertake a comprehensive retooling of everything

from product to packaging. The company reformulated many of its products — replete with sustainable, certified-organic and wildcrafted ingredients — to earn ECOCERT certification, while Elixir developed the elevator pitch and redesign of Naturopathica's brand visual language — including identity, business system, style guide and packaging for nearly 100 products.

Designers: Scott Hesselink, Holly Holmquist
Creative Director: Jennifer Jerde

NATUROPATHICA®

74 MONTAUK HIGHWAY   EAST HAMPTON   NEW YORK   11937   TEL 631.329.8792   FAX 631.329.2195   NATUROPATHICA.COM

The Kaknäs Tower

This is a school project that began as a typographic exercise and was later developed into a visual identity. The Kaknäs tower is one of Sweden's most important broadcasting masts and has been part of the Stockholm skyline since 1963. An abstracted representation of the tower's concrete structure was the basis of the logo for the project, while the colour palette was also derived from the architectural object.

The burnished gold accent colour was inspired by the gold-tinted windows of the panoramic restaurant at the top of the tower. The designer chose Univers as the main typeface – it was designed during the same era as the tower and in the case of both items, their elegance has not faded over the intervening years.

THE KAKNÄS
TOWER

THE KAKNÄS
TOWER

STEFAN MÖLLER
CEO

⁺46 709-94 75 64
stefan.moller@kaknastornet.se

Phone: ⁺46 8-667 21 05
Fax: ⁺46 8-667 85 07

Mörka Kroken 28–30
115 27 Stockholm
www.kaknastornet.se

THE KAKNÄS
TOWER

FIFTY YEARS
1963——————2013

Phone: ⁺46 (0)8 667 21 05
Fax: ⁺46 (0)8 667 85 07

Mörka Kroken 28–30
115 27 Stockholm

www.kaknastornet.se

HELLO! 32

ABCDEFGHIJKLMNOPQRSTUVXYZÅÄÖ
0123456789

THE KAKNÄS
TOWER

Sicetres

Visual identity for Sicetres, a construction
company based in Barcelona.

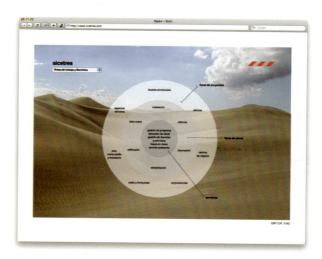

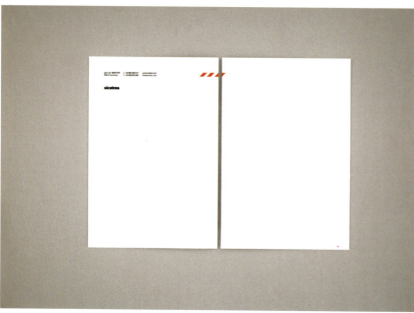

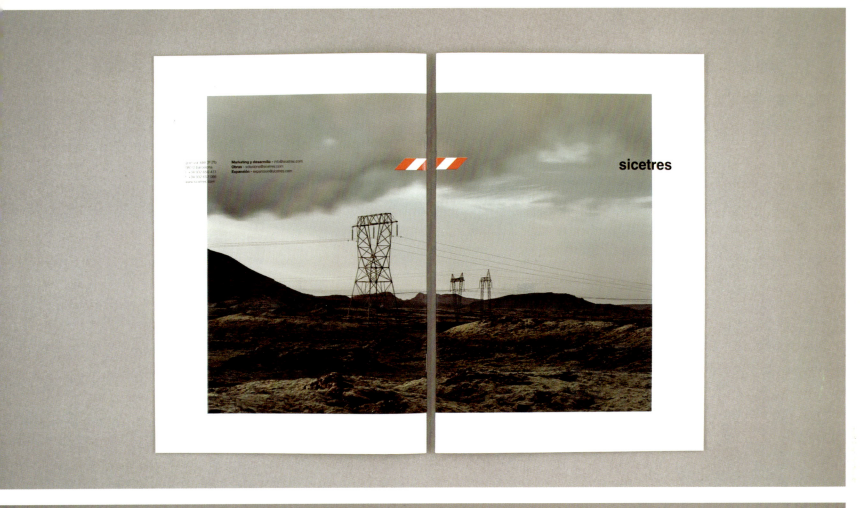

Mesoestetic Seasons

Strategy, naming and visual identity for Meso-
estetic's seasonsprogram cosmetics range.

seasonsprogram

mesoestetic®

Gabrielle Shaw Communcations

In their 10th anniversary year, Gabrielle Shaw Communications asked Fridge Creative to re-brand their company image to celebrate their growth and established reputation.

The typographic solution uses American Typewriter Light, with extra flourishes to create a stylish solution.

The illustrative tree logo is used as a mark and also as a branding tool for all printed and on-line collateral. It represents the journey that Gabrielle Shaw Communications has taken over their first 10 years, starting as an acorn and growing into a full tree. Each section of the tree has been carefully illustrated to reveal

more about the company.

The work also included a full range of print and web materials which utilised the brand identity Fridge Creative created.

The print items included a bespoke wallet brochure pack for prospective clients. Its air of polished luxury was achieved through the use of textured paper stock and die cut leaves through which the distinctive brand colours were visble, printed on the interior page of the brochure, and their contrast with the clean white of the paper could be fully appreciated.

gabrielle
shaw
communications

Fridge Creative

Shaziana

Shaziana is a banqueting and event management company which believes that everyone is unique and that events should be managed in a bespoke way to meet their clients' personal requirements.

Fridge Creative were asked to re-brand the company identity to represent their creativity and eastern influences. This work was then applied to a range of print and online materials.

Genau Messen - Herrschaft Verorten

Poster and flyer for an exhibition in Saxony,
Germany, about the history of measuring
instruments.

The aim of the participation of the Greek Foundation of Book Publishers and Booksellers in the Istanbul Book Fair 2005 was to repressent Greek cultural influences in the book market.

The concept of this series of posters was to represent the book as tactile communication medium, the key to a sensory process which opens us to our own personal exploration of the literary world. The Greek lettering used expresses Greek culture in the fields of publishing, book design and typography.

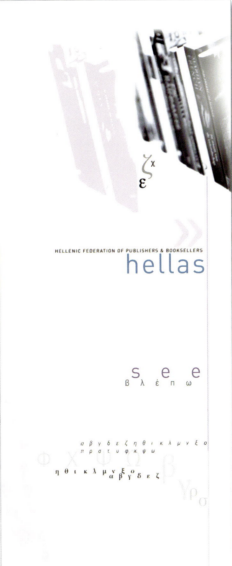

xWare

xWare is a consulting and professional inter-active development agency that specializes in developing content management systems.
The brand identity reflects their professional approach to the development of interactive media in an innovative and dynamic way, while at the same time expressing ruggedness and security, through the tight curves and powerful elements.

Peter H. Lange
phl@xware.dk
Mob — +45 6170 6600

xWare ApS
Søndergade 40-42. 2 sal
Tel — +45 7025 6025

cms@xware.dk
www.xware.dk

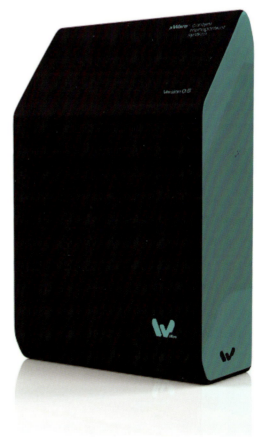

Inscape

Inscape Consulting Group is a company that specializes in leadership development and executive coaching. The die cut hole in both the business card and letterhead are an oblique reference to the power within us that is waiting to be unlocked.

Creative Director: Sean Carter
Designer: Sean Carter
Art Direction: Vida Jurcic
Production: Joan Hunter
Copywriter: Nigel Yonge

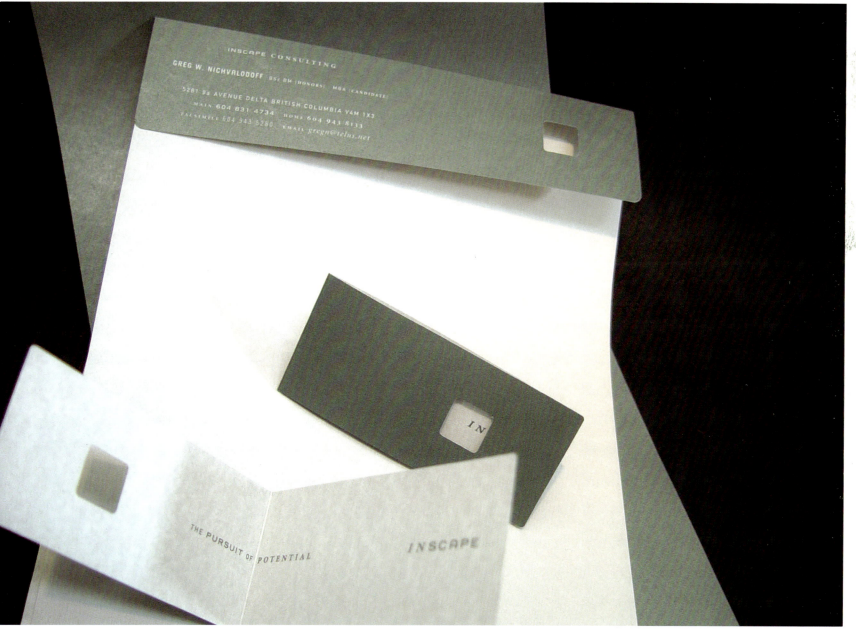

Strativity

Strativity specializes in helping service organizations deliver enhanced customer experiences. The stationery developed by Hangar 18 suggests the chemistry required to accomplish this. Various colours were used in the stationery package to add variety.

Creative Director: Sean Carter
Designer: Sean Carter
Art Direction: Sophie Frøysaa
Production: Joan Hunter
Copywriter: Nigel Yonge

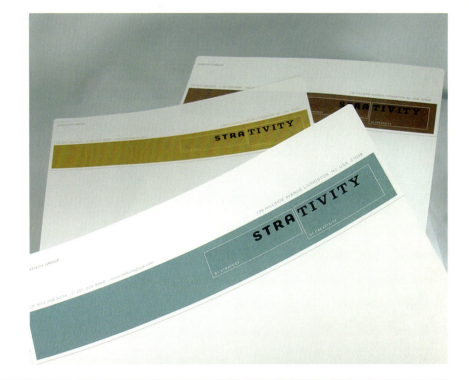

Hangar 18

Pink Door Paper Company

The Pink Door Paper Company produces stationery and soaps ornately packaged in pleasing patterns and finely textured paper stock.

Creative Director: Sean Carter
Designer: Sean Carter
Art Direction: Vida Jurcic
Production: Joan Hunter
Copywriter: Nigel Yonge

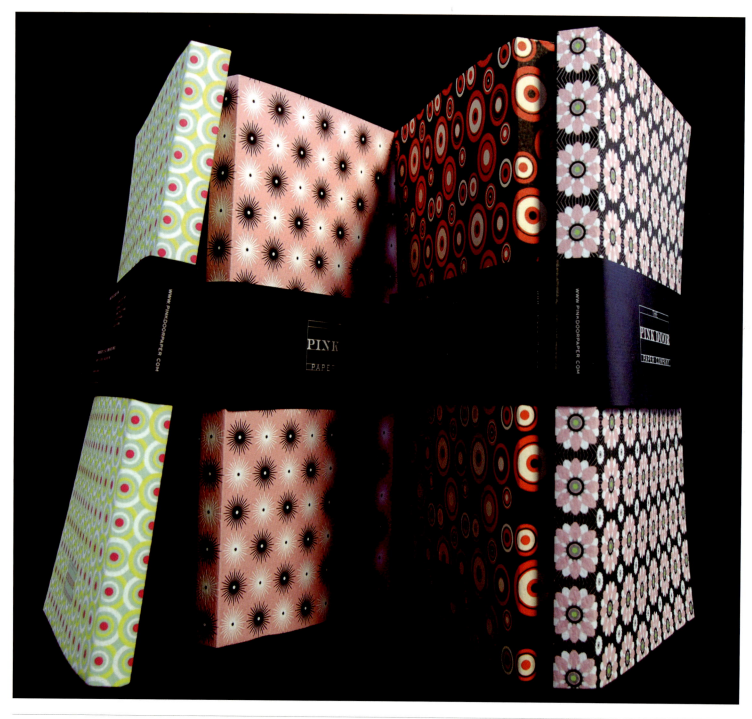

Hangar 18

Charles' Chocolates

When renowned San Francisco chocolatier Charles Siegel decided to create a small, gourmet collection bearing his name, he needed a corporate identity and e-commerce website every bit as delicious as his delectable confections. He turned to Hatch.

The logo and packaging they created can now be seen in more than 1200 gourmet fooderies across the country. The e-commerce website now serves as a primary consumer portal into the delectable world of this artisan dark chocolate.

"The team at Hatch was able to transform the seemingly impossible mandate – to create a look that is both sophisticated and whimsical – into a design that has been integral to our success. In addition to winning awards and being published in multiple design magazines, the designs have helped us grow my kitchen to a state-of-the-art 12 000 sqft kitchen with distribution to specialty food retailers nationwide." Chuck Siegel, Founder, Charles' Chocolates

Designer: Eszter T. Clark
Art Direction: Joel Templin

Coldwater Prawns of Norway

Three former competitors with long experience of prawn fishing teamed up to create a joint sales and marketing company under the name of Coldwater Prawns of Norway. The company's boats account for about 80% of all shrimp that are caught by Norwegian ocean-going vessels. Coldwater Prawns of Norway enters the future with one of the finest, purest and healthiest product in the world. The company were also recently announced Official Associated Member of Bocuse d'Or.

Art director, graphic design: Tom Emil Olsen
Communications advisor: Anders Møller
Havnevik

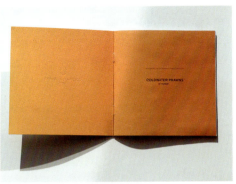

Havnevik

Concept Bridge

Visual identity for the maritime turnkey bridge system, ConceptBridge, which is a sub-brand of the Havyard Group.

Art director, graphic design: Tom Emil Olsen
Communications advisor: Anders Møller
Havnevik

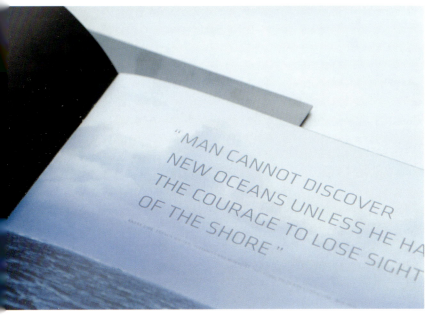

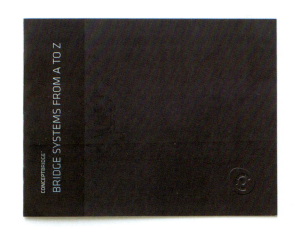

Farstad Shipping ASA

Havnevik designed this award-winning book for the 50th anniversary of Farstad Shipping ASA. Farstad is a major international supplier of large, modern offshore support vessels. The company's headquarters are located in Aalesund on the northwestern coast of Norway. Farstad Shipping also has offices in Aberdeen (Scotland), Melbourne (Australia), Singapore and in Macaé (Brazil). Through a joint venture they also have a presence in Angola. The total number of shore personnel is 160 and the number of sailors is around 1700. Farstad Shipping has a fleet of approximately 60 vessels and more vessels under construction.

Embossed on the cover of the book are the names of all the fleets from the company's first fifty years. The book received the gold award in the Norwegian advertising competition "Sterk Reklame" ("Strong Advertising") in 2010.

Art director, graphic design: Tom Emil Olsen and Robert Dalen
Assistant AD: Lise Marie Bjørge
Communications advisor: Anders Møller
Havnevik

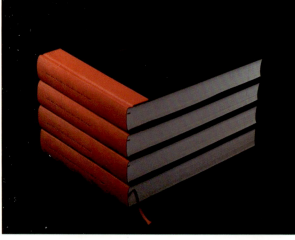

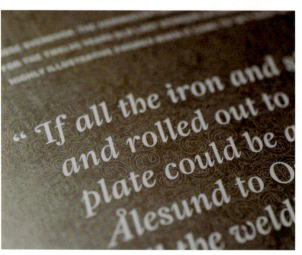

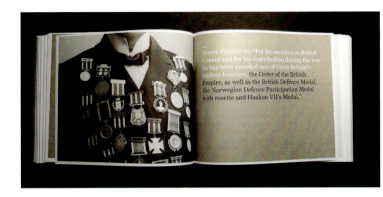

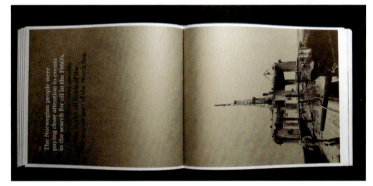

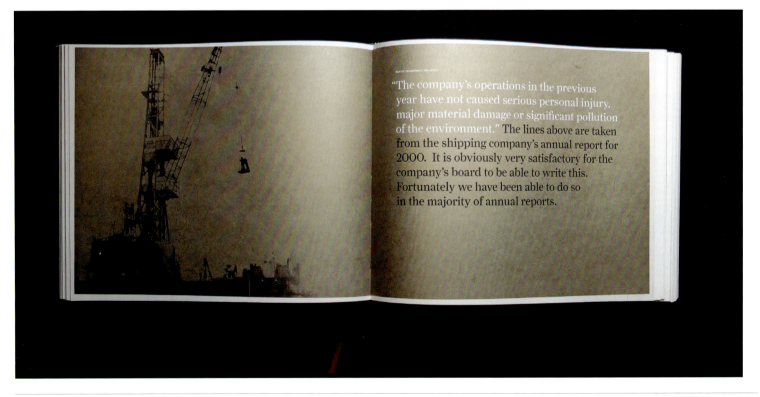

Grøvik Verk

This award-winning book was developed for the 50th anniversary of Norway's leading manufacturer of gutter systems.

The book was awarded gold in the highest ranked book-design award in Norway, "Årets vakreste bøker" ("The most beautiful books of the year"). The award is delivered by "Grafill" (The Norwegian Organization for Visual Communication). The jury commented: "a heart warming and well-founded anniversary volume that captures the feel of past eras. Fantastic portraits and picture stories from the company's history"

The book was also exhibited in the world¹s largest trade fair for books, "the Frankfurt Book Fair", and the European book esibition in Leipzig "Die Schönsten Bücher der Welt" ("The most beautiful books in the world").

Grøvik Verk is Norway's leading manufacturer of gutter systems, and its only producer of aluminum gutters. Grøvik gutter systems are easy to install, strong, durable and very competitive in price. The first gutter was installed in 1956 and is still in perfect working order today.

Art director, graphic design: Tom Emil Olsen
Communications advisor: Thomas Olai Thomassen

Ein gründers verk

"Dunderhoff" og "Vidlanna"

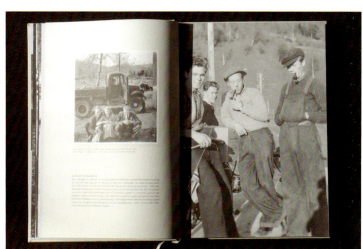

1960

"Eg var ikkje gamle karen
før eg vart med far og bestefar
på dorging og linefiske"

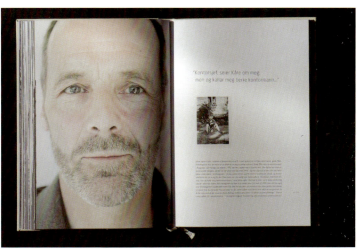

"Kontorsjef, seier Kåre om meg,
men eg kallar meg berre kontormann..."

Surofi

This project constituted the rebranding or conceptual branding of a 65-year-old visual identity. SUROFI, a fishing sales organization, was founded on 24th July 1945, and is today the second largest sales organization in the white fish sector in Norway. SUROFI have a monopoly on all first sales of white fish and shellfish in their district in west of Norway.

Art director, graphic design: Tom Emil Olsen
Communications advisor: Thomas Olai Thomassen

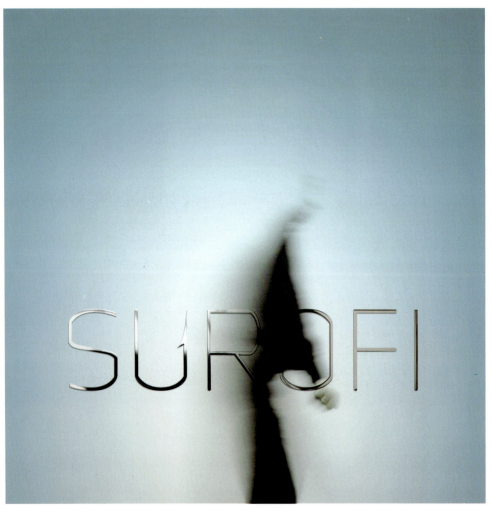

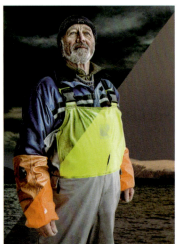

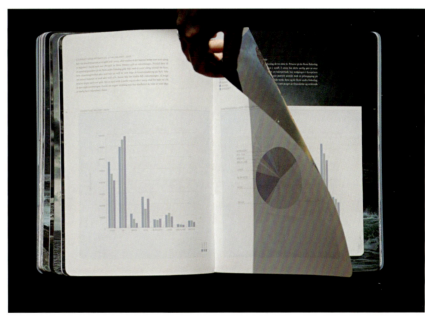

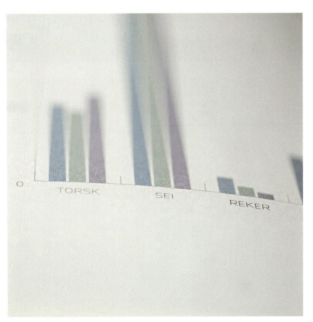

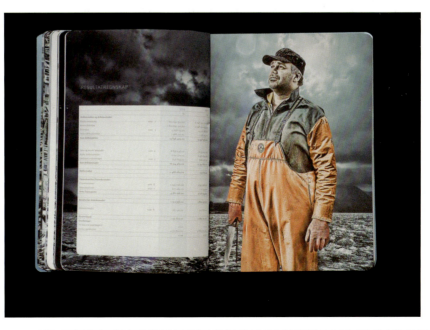

Floresta

fLorEsta is a florist located in Long Island City, NY. HI(NY) was asked to create a brand identity along with the collateral items such as shopping bags, candle packaging and signage.

Art Direction, Graphic Design: Hitomi Watanabe, Iku Oyamada

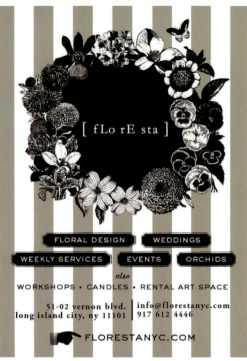

Hector & Hoodini

Hector & Hoodini is a New York-based leather goods label. HI(NY) was asked to create a brand identity along with collateral items such as a zipper pull, labels and the pattern for lining fabric.

Art Direction, Graphic Design: Hitomi Watanabe, Iku Oyamada

North Star Fund 2010 Community Gala

North Star Fund is an established New York community foundation supporting grassroots groups leading the movement for equality, economic justice, and peace. Every year at the North Star Fund Community Gala, donors and grantees come together to celebrate the work of philanthropic and community activists, and North Star Fund's role in bringing them together. Hyperakt was tasked with developing branding for the event, including save-the-date cards, printed and interactive invitations, the event program, and event signage.

Creative Direction & Design: Julia Vakser
Design: Deroy Peraza, Jason Lynch

Hyperakt

North Star Fund 2010 Annual Report

North Star Fund's 2010 Annual Report, their fourth designed by Hyperakt, is all about the leaders of their donor community. Their inspiring diverse backgrounds are the guiding light for North Star Fund's quest to create an equitable and peaceful New York City.

Creative Direction: Julia Vakser & Deroy Peraza
Design: Jason Lynch

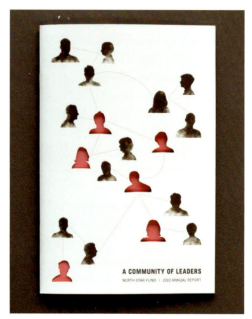

KATRINA SCHAFFER

I grew up in the suburbs of Kansas City, Missouri. They are very quiet, very conservative. But I credit my parents, especially my mother, for giving me a different perspective about the world. My mom grew up in the countryside of Germany. She came to the United States because she wanted a better life as a woman than the one that was presented to her there. Alongside that, my youngest sister is a person with cerebral palsy and other special needs. Growing up, I watched my mother and father become advocates for my sister's life and watched my sister's determination and ambition to lead the life she wants come up against the way society treats people with special needs. My mom also instilled in me the values of kindness and patience, of being able to listen to people and hear their experience, of bringing passion and heart to my work and the issues I care about. Thanks to her, and my whole family, I can see issues that affect my own life, and then relate those to issues that affect other people more directly.

Since the first day that I stepped into New York City, I've heard North Star Fund's name. Over and over, I found that the most exciting work that was being done in New York had received both start-up funding and continuing support from North Star. So when I was ready to be more involved with supporting local efforts, North Star Fund was the first group I turned to.

Members and staff of Rights for Imprisoned People with Psychiatric Disabilities (RIPPD) before a rally at City Hall Park. Credit: Amy Ponce

OUR EXPANDED GRANTMAKING VISION

Building Leadership & Movements

"For many years, North Star Fund has helped to seed innovative new projects that other funders wouldn't take the risk on. As a result, the groups we have supported have become stronger and more effective base-building community organizing groups. With these new guidelines, North Star can support groups at multiple stages of their development—not just start-ups."

—Kevin Ryan
North Star Fund board member
Program Officer, New York Foundation

2010 GRANT CATEGORIES

Grassroots Action Grants North Star Fund will continue to award half of our activist-led grantmaking dollars as grants of $5,000 and $10,000 to new, emerging groups who are reaching out through the tools of community organizing to engage more community people as leaders and grassroots activists in New York City's most marginalized communities.

Movement Leadership Grants A centerpiece of our new grants vision, $50,000 grants over two years will make a deeper investment of general support in effective organizations that have already shown a strong record of success in their community organizing work.

Innovative Activism Grants A new grant category that continues a hallmark of North Star's support for grassroots groups, these $10,000 grants will support social justice work beyond community organizing including cultural, art and media projects, as well as resources for activism and community organizing.

Grassroots Strategy Grants Another new category, members of our community funding committee will now be able to invest in a great campaign idea to achieve concrete change. These $15,000 grants will enable groups to access additional research, legal, media, policy and organizing expertise at a critical strategic moment.

10

11

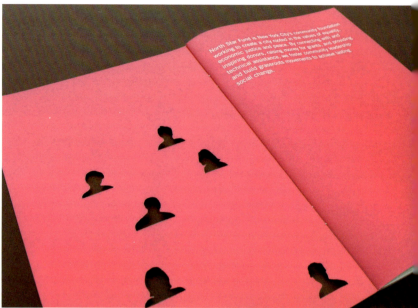

North Star Fund is New York City's community foundation working to create a city rooted in the values of equality, economic justice and peace. By connecting with, and inspiring donors, raising money for grants, and providing technical assistance, we foster community leadership and build grassroots movements to achieve lasting social change.

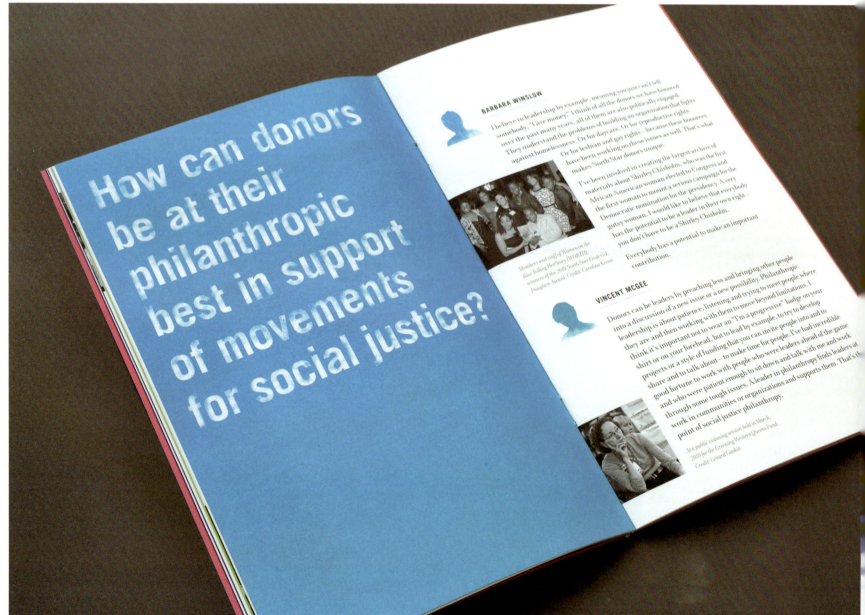

How can donors be at their philanthropic best in support of movements for social justice?

BARBARA WINSLOW

I believe in leadership by example, meaning you just can't tell somebody, "Give money." I think of all the donors we have honored over the past many years, all of them are also politically engaged. They understand the problems of building an organization that fights against homelessness. Or for daycare. Or for reproductive rights. Or for lesbian and gay rights — because these honorees have been working on these issues as well. That's what makes North Star donors unique.

I've been involved in creating the largest archive of materials about Shirley Chisholm, who was the first African-American woman elected to Congress and the first woman to mount a serious campaign for the Democratic nomination for the presidency. A very gutsy woman. I would like to believe that everybody has the potential to be a leader in their own right — you don't have to be a Shirley Chisholm.

Everybody has a potential to make an important contribution.

Members and staff of Women on the Rise Telling HerStory (WORTH), winners of the 2010 North Star Frederick Douglass Award. Credit: Carolina Kroon

VINCENT MCGEE

Donors can be leaders by preaching less and bringing other people into a discussion of a new issue or a new possibility. Philanthropic leadership is about patience, listening and trying to meet people where they are and then working with them to move beyond limitations. I think it's important not to wear an "I'm a progressive" badge on your shirt or on your forehead, but to lead by example, to try to develop projects or a style of funding that you can invite people into and to share and to talk about — to make time for people. I've had incredible good fortune to work with people who were leaders ahead of the game and who were patient enough to sit down and talk with me and work through some tough issues. A leader in philanthropy finds leaders at work in communities or organizations and supports them. That's the point of social justice philanthropy.

At a public training session held in March, 2010 for the Greening Western Queens Fund. Credit: Gerard Gaskin

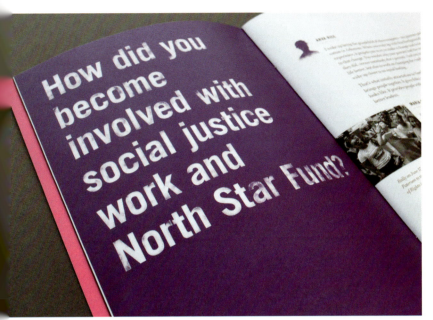

How did you become involved with social justice work and North Star Fund?

How does North Star Fund contribute to a better New York City?

* *Temporarily Restricted Net Assets:*
North Star Fund receives donor advised contributions that are held until donors recommend which organizations will receive grants.

INCOME

Individual Donors
$1,960,220
31%

Fees and Investments
$222,590
4%

Foundation Partners
$175,000
3%

Donor Advised Partners *
$3,899,270
62%

EXPENSES

Grants and Programs
$1,105,589
37%

Management and General
$186,640
6%

Development
$232,607
8%

Donor Advised Grants
$1,453,950
49%

NORTH STAR FUND GRANTMAKING

	Activist-Led Grants	Donor Advised Grants
2003	$311,469	$17,500
2004	$304,050	$21,500
2005	$380,000	$91,000
2006	$366,335	$656,960
2007	$463,840	$144,950
2008	$504,450	$1,170,041
2009	$517,277	$1,330,988
2010	$535,491	$1,453,950

*During the year ended June 30, 2008, North Star Fund entered into an agreement with a donor advised partner who was interested in making large grants in the South Bronx. This three-year partnership brought significant resources to a marginalized area of New York City. During the year ended June 30, 2010, the New York State Public Service Commission selected North Star Fund as Greening Projects Administrator to develop a grantmaking program that will result in nearly $7.9 million in grants to green the infrastructure of neighborhoods in Western Queens.

The White House Project: Epic Awards

The White House Project's 2010 EPIC Awards are a celebration of women's leadership in the media and in popular culture. The April 7th, 2010 event took place at the IAC Building in New York City, designed by Frank Gehry. Among those in attendance were Meryl Streep, Jill Scott, Gina Davis, and Megan Mullally. Several awards were presented to women making a positive impact through art and activism, including the Global Trailblazer Award honoring Kiran Bedi, Indian social activist and Asia Nobel Prize winner.

All graphics for the event were designed by Hyperakt, including invitations, place cards, wall graphics, dinner menus, and keynote presentations. Check out pictures from the event on Flickr.

Tiffany Dufu, WHP's Vice President of Development and Administration called the work *"just stunning"*. *"Every member of the WHP staff that has worked with you all raves about your skill, flexibility, creativity and especially how nice and cool you both are. I think WHP and Hyperakt is a match made in heaven and I can't thank you enough for you efforts in making our 2010 EPIC awards a success."*
Kristina Goodman, WHP's Director of PR and Marketing and Breann Peterson, WHP's Development Coordinator said *"The IAC building has never looked better because of your creative genius!"*

Creative Direction & Design: Julia Vakser, Deroy Peraza
Design: Jason Lynch

Global Humanitarian Assistance

Hype & Slippers was approached by Global Humanitarian Assistance to align their identity and produce their 2010 report and new website. Taking their existing logo as a basis, the designers delivered an identity which was slick, consistent and most crucially, engaging. Heavily data driven, GHA's printed materials and online presence needed to be clear and concise a friendly info-graphic style was developed to satisfy these requirements.

Hype & Slippers were also commissioned to produce 12 info-graphics to communicate key findings and figures. Designed in line with the new identity, these info-graphics became an important tool for the organisation.

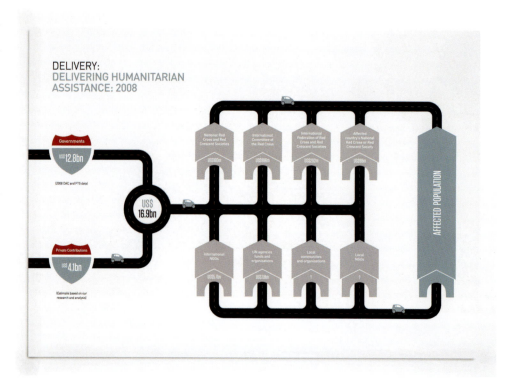

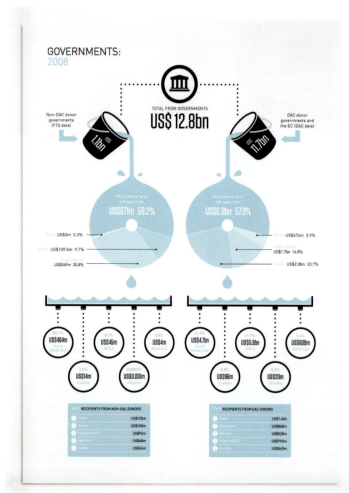

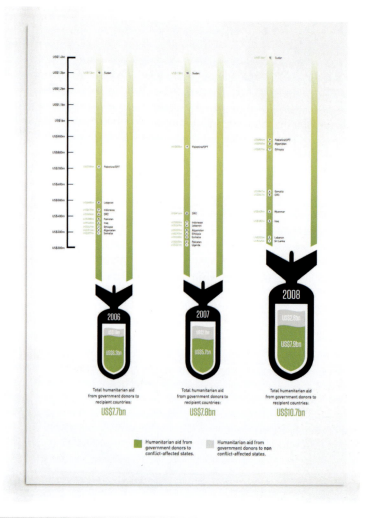

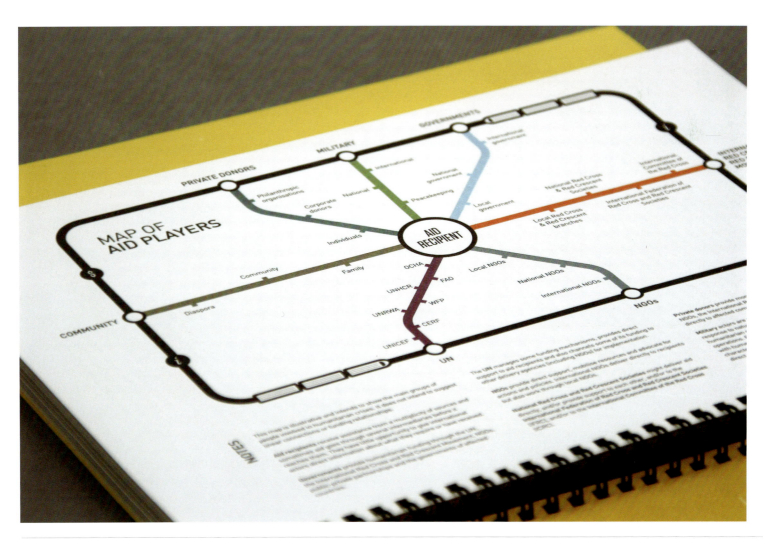

Dolphin Square

Dolphin Square is a renowned residential development in Pimlico, London. A complete renovation of the building signalled the need for a thorough re-branding programme. A period of two and half years saw an intense schedule of creative and production work, leading to over 180 separate design projects. A comprehensive brand structure was required to manage the multitude of brand applications which include the website, signage and environmental branding, advertising and the many pieces of printed marketing material.The conclusion of the branding for Dolphin Square led to the subsequent development of associated brands: Dolphin House, Dolphin Bar & Grill and Dolphin Fitness Club.

Design Director: Vivek Bhatia
Designer: Alex James
Photographer: Fernando Mañoso

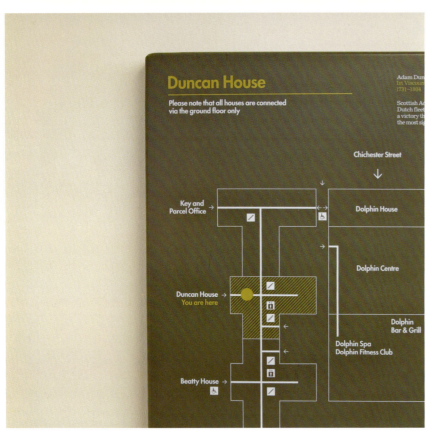

Duncan House

Please note that all houses are connected
via the ground floor only

Adam Dunc[...]
1st Viscoun[...]
1731–1804

Scottish Ad[...]
Dutch fleet[...]
a victory th[...]
the most sig[...]

Chichester Street

Key and
Parcel Office →

Dolphin House

Dolphin Centre

Duncan House
You are here

Dolphin
Bar & Grill

Dolphin Spa
Dolphin Fitness Club

Beatty House

Dolphin
Square SW1

330ml

Refreshingly affordable

Dolp
Squ

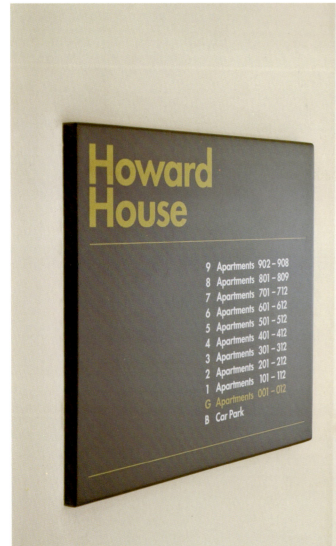

Howard
House

9 Apartments 902 – 908
8 Apartments 801 – 809
7 Apartments 701 – 712
6 Apartments 601 – 612
5 Apartments 501 – 512
4 Apartments 401 – 412
3 Apartments 301 – 312
2 Apartments 201 – 212
1 Apartments 101 – 112
G Apartments 001 – 012
B Car Park

The Chemistry Centre

The Chemistry Centre is a new public space comprising a library and events centre, run by the Royal Society of Chemistry in Burlington House on Piccadilly. The new brand celebrates the excitement of chemistry past, present and future with a contemporary and engaging graphic language, while maintaining an authoritative demeanour. In addition to a new logotype and a bold colour palette, a central ingredient of the brand identity is an infinitely flexible graphic device based on rudimentary Bohr atom symbols. The brand strategy called for increased public awareness; the consistent copy structure for headlines that read "...at The Chemistry Centre", enables emphasis to be placed on the brand name in all communications.

What's on
at_The
Chemistry
Centre

Get involved
at_The
Chemistry
Centre

Impress
your audience
at_The
Chemistry
Centre

Chocolate
at_The
Chemistry
Centre

Fireworks
at_The
Chemistry
Centre

Robert Boyle
A retrospective
at_The
Chemistry
Centre

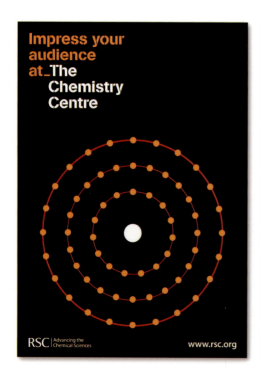

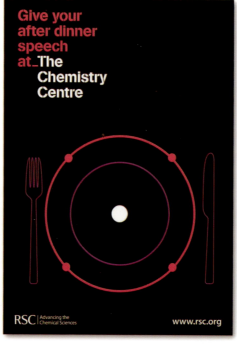

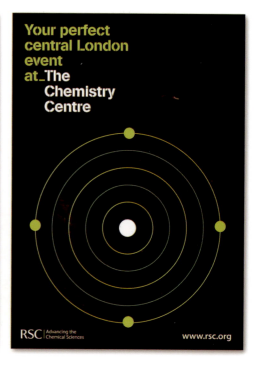

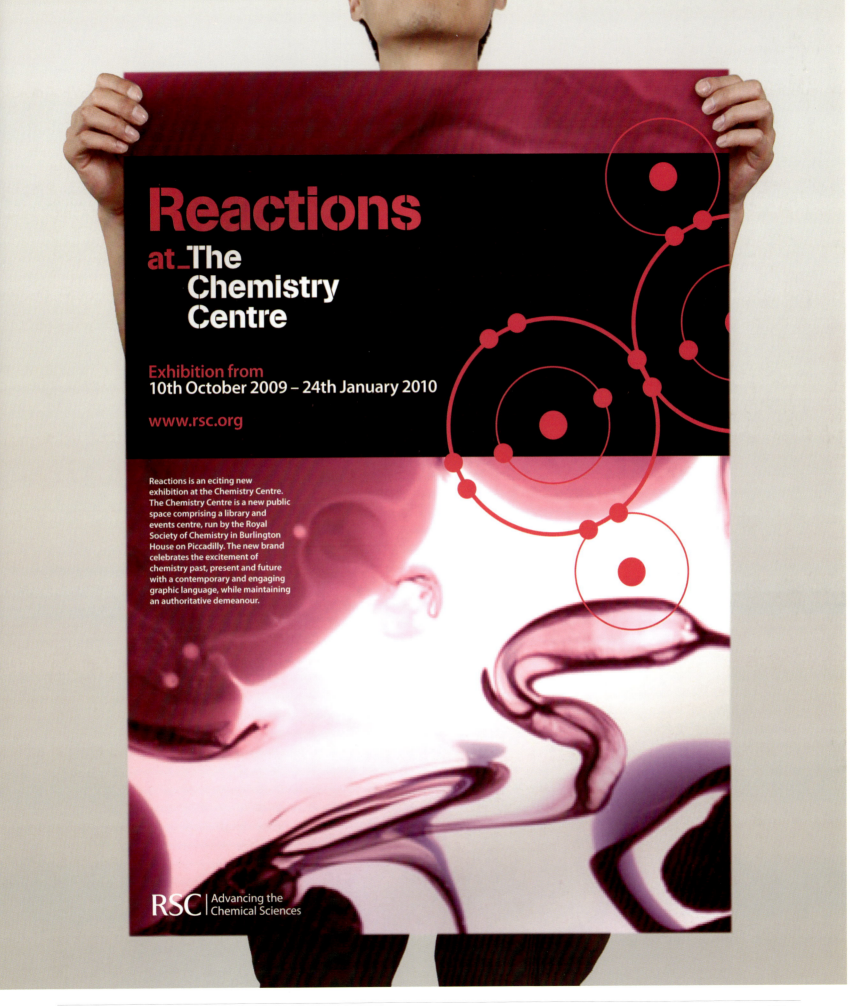

ico Design

Total Office

Total Office is an established, independent London based office supply company. On merging with another operator, they identified the need for a brand overhaul. Their name expresses the comprehensiveness of their catalogue of office supplies. However, in reality, they are able to supply much more than just office products. They have a proactive team that aims to help customers with any request. The strapline 'Totally possible' confidently communicates this flexibility. The 'from x to y' concept further reinforces this idea; illustrations of everyday objects juxtaposed with some more unexpected items visually demonstrates the scope of their customer offering. A consciously contemporary graphic style, together with a fresh colour palette, helps raise the perception of the company within the marketplace.

Design Director: Vivek Bhatia
Designer: Alex James
Writer: Gerard Ivall

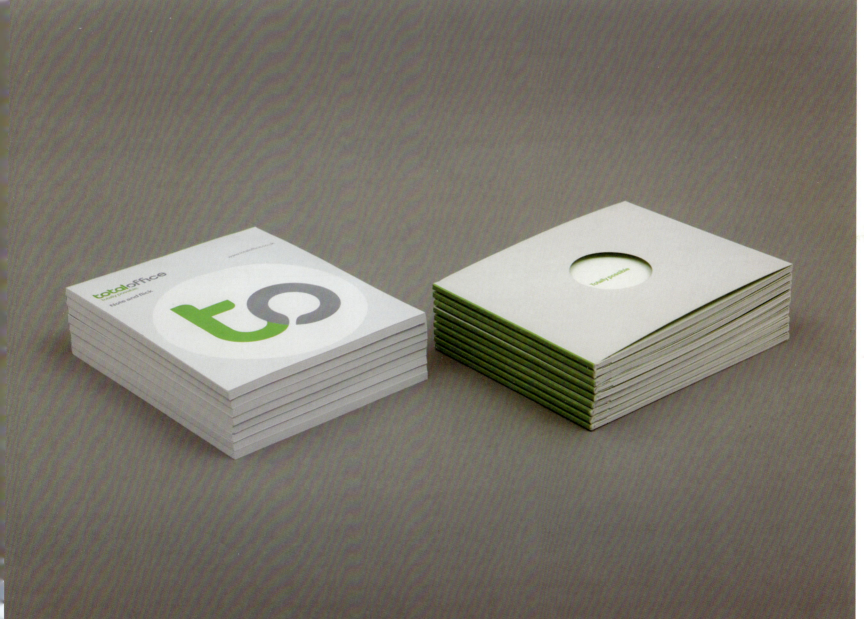

Neolab corporate identity

Neolab is an IT company specializing in building business information systems, web applications and websites. Taking inspiration from Neolab's work creating and connecting web environments, IlovarStritar designed a corporate identity based on the idea of an open, developing ecosystem.

The elements of the "ecosystem" have two common characteristics:

1. The fusion of various existing elements to create a new one, a metaphor for merging technologies and business systems.

2. Progressive pixelization from left to right, conveying Neolab's internet operations.

Various motifs combine with the Neolab text to form the logo. The motifs all have metaphorical meanings, such as the combination of a pigeon with a cheetah for the envelope design (postal service + speed).

Creative Director: Robert Ilovar
Designer: Robert Ilovar

Lundgren+Lindqvist

Apple Education Leadership Summit

Each year Apple host an Education Leadership Summit in London which coincides with BETT, the largest education technology exhibition in the world. The summit focuses on technology and learning and features high profile lecturers from around the world.

For Apple ELS 2011, Lundgren+Lindqvist designed the invitations, the printed program and a website where the visitor could find the full program and also mark what lectures or seminars they would like to attend, which was then submitted in a form along with their personal information.

The printed program was designed to work both as a teaser for the program and as an actual aid to the visitors when attending the summit. The 26-page folded program includes, beside the actual program and information about the event, a custom-desgined London map with the lecture venues marked on it along with the location of the Apple headquarters and the Mayfair Hotel, which is hosting some of the seminars as well as serving as the residence for some of the visitors. Four pages (the backsides of the day overviews), were separated into four stripes (one for each day) with the London skyline, the main graphic element of ELS 2011, moving from top to bottom to illustrate the passing of time and its contrast to the fixed state of the skyline.

The striped sky illustrates the fact that in London in January it rains every other day.

The pages of the program were perforated so that the visitor would only need to bring the program for the current day along with them during each day of the summit. The back of the program is ruled and blank for the attendees to take notes during lectures and seminars. The page also features web links.

The program was printed on 300gsm uncoated Munken stock that would withstand the wear and tear of the four-day summit.

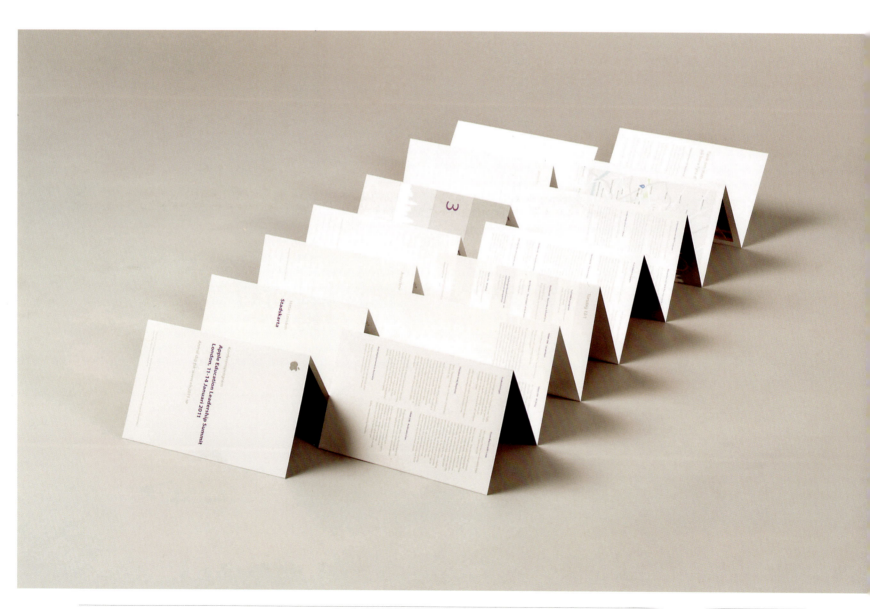

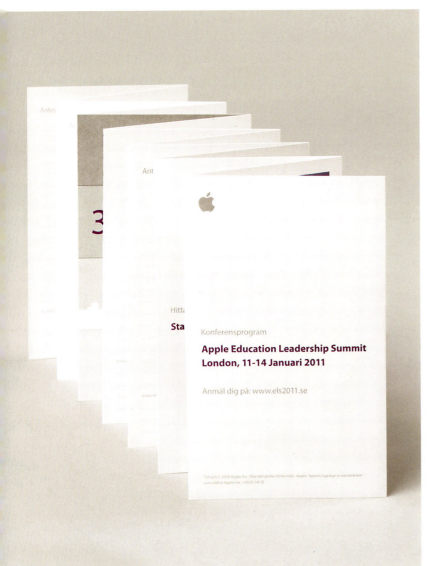

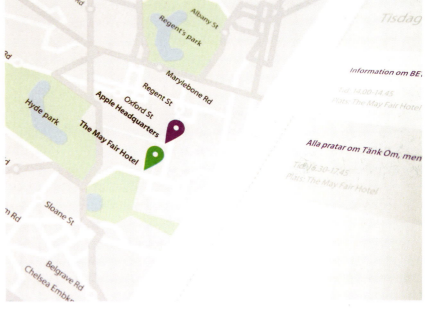

Sound Studies

The four semester master course in sound studies in the UdK Berlin gives a professional qualification for working with sound in arts and design. The intensive course is accompanied by mentors and includes four modules: sound-anthropology and sound-ecology: the theory and history of auditive culture; experimental sound design; and auditive media design. Melgrafik designed the acoustic conception and brand communication.

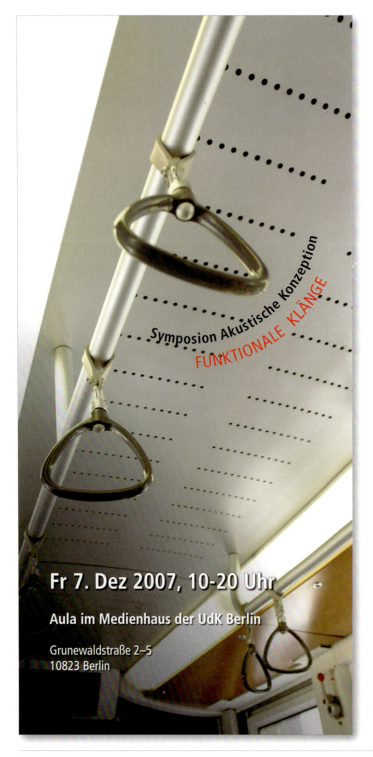

Mind Design

D100 Idenity

D100 is a modern dentistry at the Barbican (100 Aldersgate street). The identity is inspired by the raking patterns around stones in Japanese Zen gardens and the protective layers of enamel around teeth. The patterns have also been applied to the interior in concentric rings around the furniture and various fixed or removable objects in the practice.

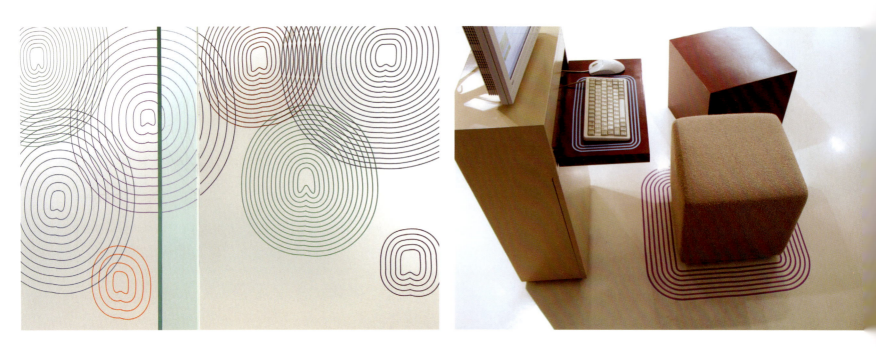

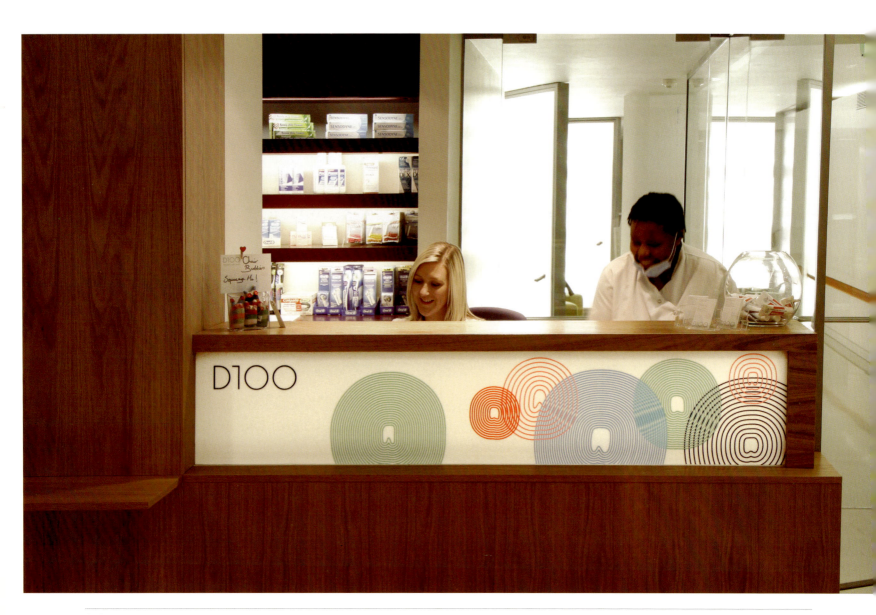

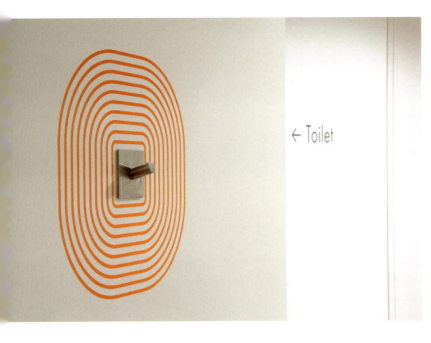

← Toilet

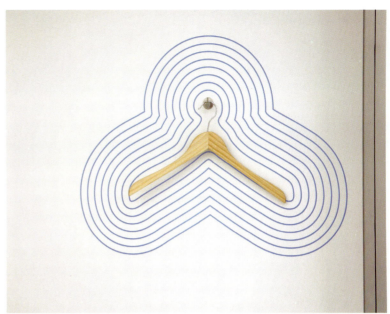

Tea

Identity and overall design concept for a chain of tea shops, simply called 'Tea'. The first shop is located next to Saint Paul's Cathedral in London, a popular tourist destination.

The idea of the logo is that the inner part of the letter 'a' forms the tea leaf and changes colour according to the type of tea. The colour scheme is used to categorise similar types of tea and make the rather complex world of tea more accessible. The identity has been applied to packaging, menus and interior graphics. The clean typographic design is also used to customize traditional elements from English tea culture such as tea cozies and doilies.

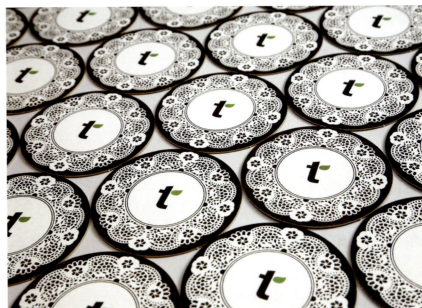

Tess Management Identity

Identity for a London based modelling agency. Tess represents well established names such as Naomi Campbell and Erin O'Connor in the UK. The identity uses several logo variations based on a modular system of Art Deco-inspired elements. The same elements are being used for frames (which overlap images of the models) on various printed applications and on the website.

In collaboration with Simon Egli, Zurich

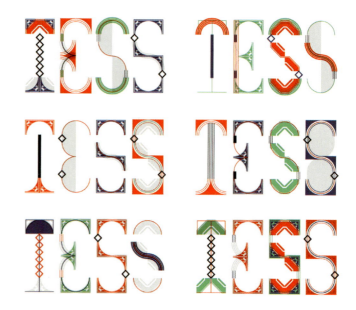

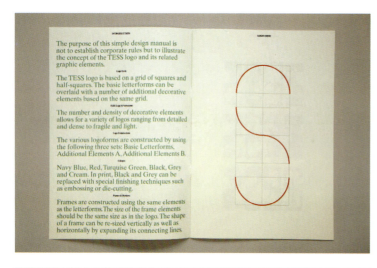

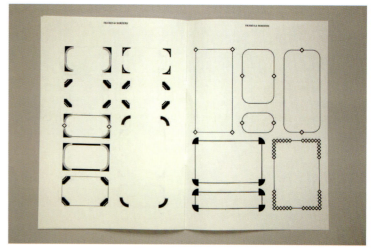

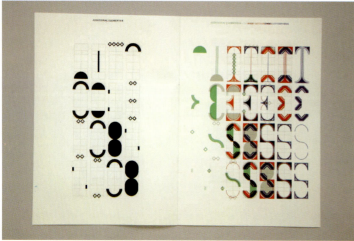

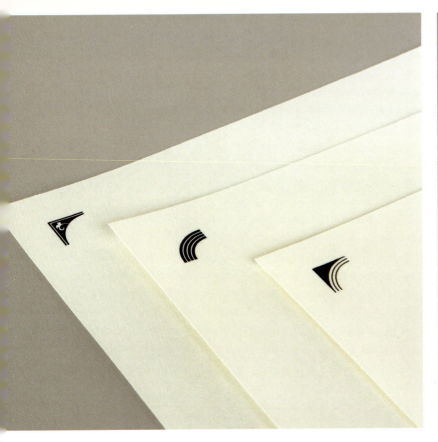

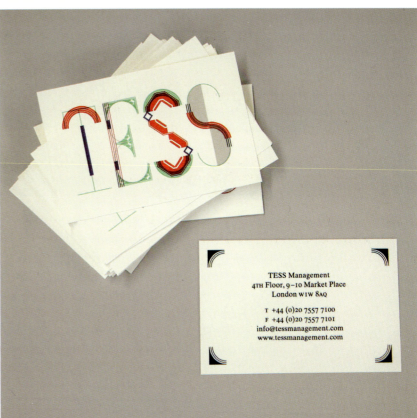

TESS Management
4TH Floor, 9–10 Market Place
London W1W 8AQ

T +44 (0)20 7557 7100
F +44 (0)20 7557 7101
info@tessmanagement.com
www.tessmanagement.com

Russell Marsh Casting

Russell Marsh casts models for fashion shows and photo shoots. Since his ability is to spot perfection and beauty in people, the identity is based on the golden section, the most perfect and beautiful proportions in design. Various line patterns related to the golden section were used on all printed material. The overlapping lines create different densities and connect at the edges of the format. The identity works without an actual logo, combining the graphic patterns with minimal and classic typography.

Russell Marsh Casting

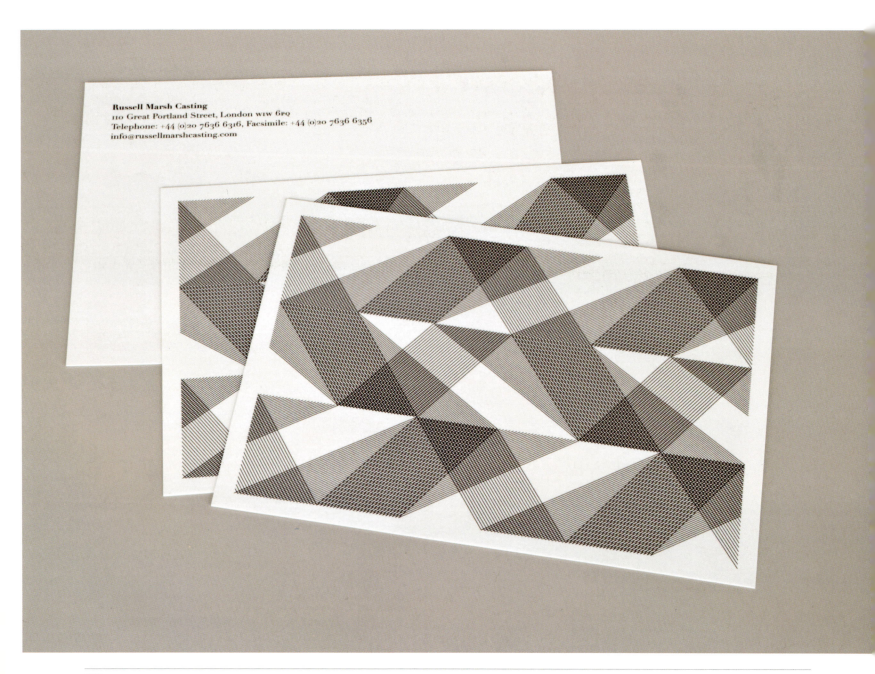

Mission Design

EDB

EDB helps companies to become more effective through IT. When a multinational bank wants to develop mobile banking and all the complexities that come with it, they call EDB.

Most of their business occurs behind closed doors. Consequently the business needed to become more visible.

Mission Design avoided typical shots of engineers in server rooms and adopted mountains as a metaphor for the firm's ability to solve ambitious tasks. This became part of a comprehensive identity programme.

Dr. Schilchegger Rechtsanwaltsgesellschafft

Dr. Schilchegger is a law firm in Austria with a brand identity that subverts stereotypes. The classical logo is replaced by sequences of images. Equally unconventional is their web page, which conveys the company's philosphy.

Pongauer Holzbau (Pongau woodworks) is an Austrian company that designs and builds wooden houses for private and public clients using traditional skills, while incorporating architectural and construction innovations.

The word-picture logo offers multiple readings: a building from the front, a sketch or a timber section.

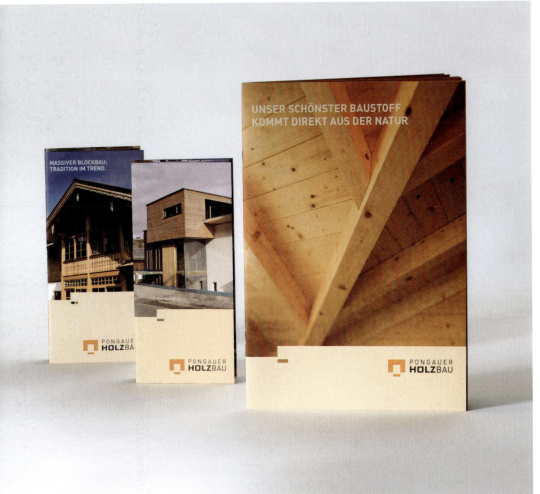

G3-Consultancy

G3-Consultancy is a business and management consultancy company with headquarters
in Austria and in Switzerland.
A clearly structured and forceful graphic character underlines the distinctiveness of G3. The
graphic language conveys the efficiency of the
organization.

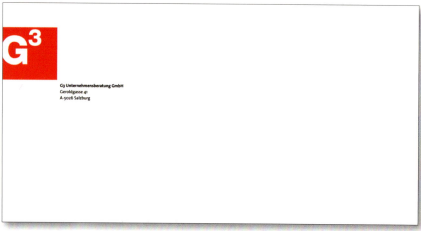

»Wir blicken unter die Oberfläche«

G³

G3 Unternehmensberatung
Wien · Salzburg · Zürich

Moving Brands worked with Norton's new Director Patrick Grant to develop an identity both respectful of the past and in tune with the present. While Nortons recognised the importance of their heritage, they wanted to continue to engage a modern generation of young customers who also appreciated fine British tailoring.

Having assessed the competition and created a customer journey for Nortons, Moving Brands began work on a new, modern identity that would acknowledge and emphasise the firm's rich heritage, while appealing to a dynamic, younger market – "the Englishman at large." The identity includes a redrawn version of Norton's original crest, which was awarded by a Prussian emperor in the 19th century. The original, idiosyncratic wordmark has also been redrawn and reinstated.

The creation of new stationery and retail material was just the first step. Moving Brands went on to design the more esoteric fineries of the Nortons experience: the clothing labels, signed by the cutters, tailors, and Patrick Grant, and stitched into each suit; passport books that chart the progress of each suit's creation; concepts for the interior design of the salon; and bespoke storage boxes for all the records, some of which date back over a century, and include invoices and patterns for Sir Winston Churchill.

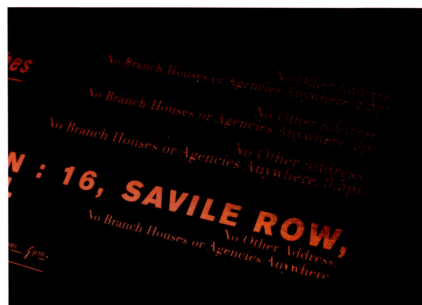

All About Tea

All About Tea is a global wholesale and retail tea distributor that prides itself on its knowledge of the world of teas and the quality of the product it brings to the consumer. All About Tea engaged Moving Brands to develop an identity system that would work effectively across their existing wholesale market, and enable them to grow into retail channels. It was also vital to communicate the founder's passion for the art and intricacies of tea.

The new identity contains the signature simplicity and straightforward approach necessary in the wholesale market, yet appeals to the retail audience by standing out in the "sea of sameness" that is evident when walking the tea aisle. The mark references the process of making tea; the blending and the straining. The symbol expresses a stamp of quality, an iconic industry standard, that represents the bold confidence inherent in their product and service.

It is a moving world identity, designed to work across all platforms. With opportunities for customers to personalize and share their own blends online, and then customize their packaging, the brand brings a new approach to the tea industry.

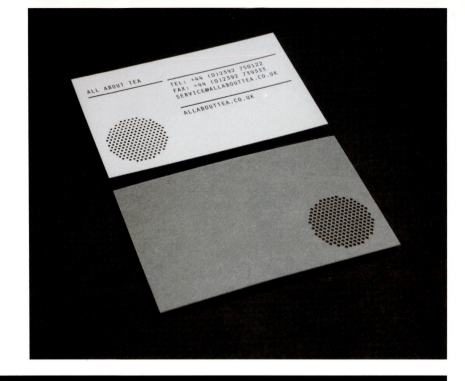

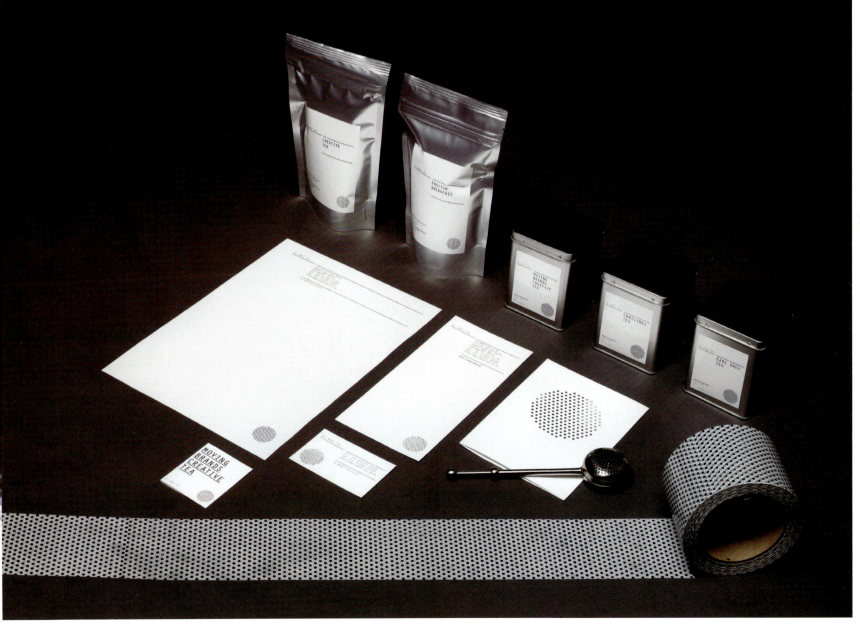

2020 Vision

A progressive leader on environmental and energy issues for over two decades, 2020 Vision sought to refocus their message and differentiate themselves in an increasingly crowded field.

Following strategic positioning workshops, a messaging platform and refreshing logo and identity system were developed. Brand extension has been implemented across all communications, establishing a progressive alternative to the oftentimes stagnant, monolithic Washington design culture.

2020 VISION
ENERGY + SECURITY SOLUTIONS

Tom Z. Collina
Executive Director

8403 Colesville Road, Suite 860   +   Telephone 301-587-1782
Silver Spring, Maryland 20910   +   Facsimile 301-587-1848
www.2020vision.org   +   tcollina@2020vision.org

IT'S TIME TO MAKE A DIFFERENCE

GET A *FREE* TRIP TO WASHINGTON—HELP LEAD A NATIONAL ADVOCACY CAMPAIGN AND BRING THE ENERGY CRISIS DEBATE TO YOUR CAMPUS.

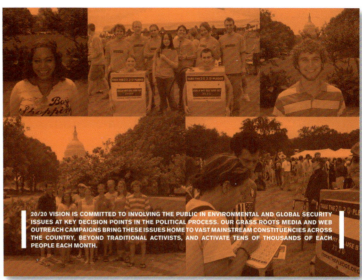

20/20 VISION IS COMMITTED TO INVOLVING THE PUBLIC IN ENVIRONMENTAL AND GLOBAL SECURITY ISSUES AT KEY DECISION POINTS IN THE POLITICAL PROCESS. OUR GRASS ROOTS MEDIA AND WEB OUTREACH CAMPAIGNS BRING THESE ISSUES HOME TO VAST MAINSTREAM CONSTITUENCIES ACROSS THE COUNTRY, BEYOND TRADITIONAL ACTIVISTS, AND ACTIVATE TENS OF THOUSANDS OF EACH PEOPLE EACH MONTH.

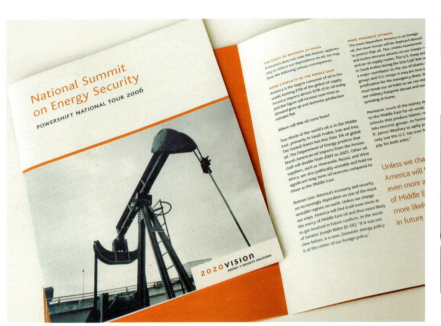

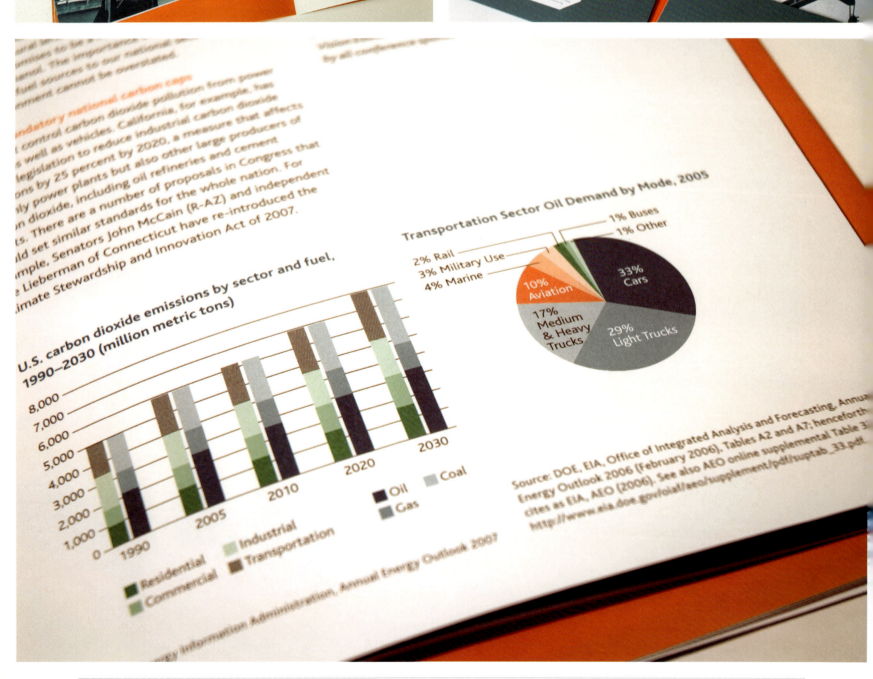

U.S. carbon dioxide emissions by sector and fuel, 1990–2030 (million metric tons)

Oil
Gas
Coal

Residential
Commercial
Industrial
Transportation

Transportation Sector Oil Demand by Mode, 2005

1% Buses
1% Other
33% Cars
29% Light Trucks
17% Medium & Heavy Trucks
10% Aviation
4% Marine
3% Military Use
2% Rail

Source: DOE, EIA, Office of Integrated Analysis and Forecasting, Annual Energy Outlook 2006 (February 2006), Tables A2 and A7; henceforth cites as EIA, AEO (2006). See also AEO online supplemental Table 33, http://www.eia.doe.gov/oiaf/aeo/supplement/pdf/suptab_33.pdf

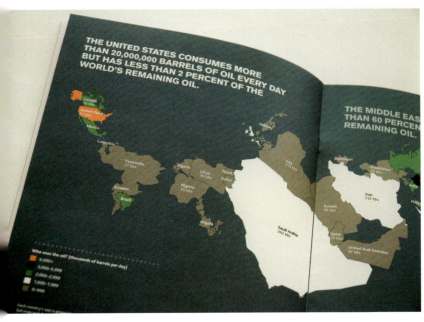

THE UNITED STATES CONSUMES MORE THAN 20,000,000 BARRELS OF OIL EVERY DAY BUT HAS LESS THAN 2 PERCENT OF THE WORLD'S REMAINING OIL.

THE MIDDLE EAST CONTROLS MORE THAN 60 PERCENT OF THE WORLD'S REMAINING OIL.

THE MIDDLE EAST CONTROLS MORE THAN 60 PERCENT OF THE WORLD'S REMAINING OIL.

SAVE THE DATE! JULY 12, 2007 FOR THE NATIONAL SUMMIT ON ENERGY SECURITY IN WASHINGTON, DC

Agency Access

Challenged as the category leader in online marketing tools for creative artists, Agency Access sought to differentiate themselves from increased competition in their specialized, niche market.

Research focused on aligning strategic goals with customer need, with a resulting Brand Handbook distilling business and brand vision to speed internal adoption of brand repositioning. Integrated identity design extends across print collateral, the company's website and an optimized interface for Agency Access' core online customer product.

BRAND TONE

WELCOMING. CREATIVE. COMPREHENSIVE. RELIABLE. CURRENT. FACILITATING. SAVVY. HIGH-QUALITY. SIMPL INNOVATIVE.

THE TONE OF THE AGENCY ACCESS BRAND REFLECTS HOW THE CO WISHES TO BE SEEN BY THE

CREATING AND MAINTAINING A C TONE FOR THE BRAND IS A STRA OF PARAMOUNT IMPORTANCE

agency access
brand and identity standards

agencyaccess

learn more *about our brand*

Mike Singer
msinger@agencyaccess.com

PHONE   631·563·5009
FAX   631·563·4695
WEB   agencyaccess.com

1556 Ocean Ave, Suite 12
Bohemia, NY 11716

agencyaccess

Create Connections

Electrification Coalition

The Electrification Coalition brings together the heads of many of the world's leading companies across the entire value chain necessary to advancing electric vehicles as the key to energy independence. Uniting clean-tech, smart-grid, energy, automotive and related industries, the Coalition's brand identity presents a united front to setting in motion the plan to electrify the U.S. transportation system.

MSDS developed a groundbreaking, 180 page report combining policy, strategy, and business case analysis to form a comprehensive vision for the future of american transportation. In just two months, the Electrification Coalition and its Roadmap debuted to overwhelming acclaim, recording double the demand for previous publications in the first few weeks alone.

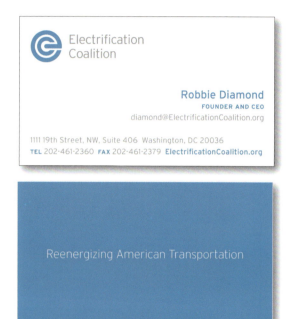

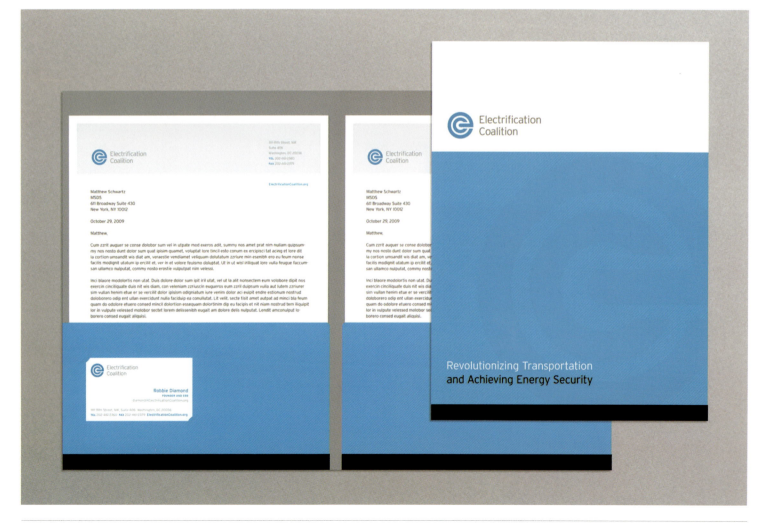

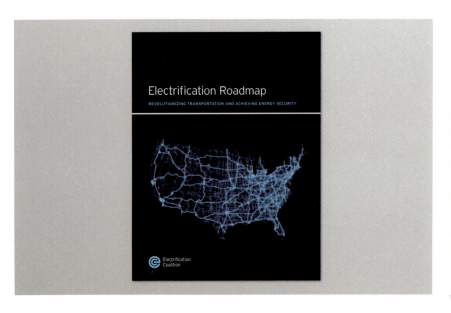

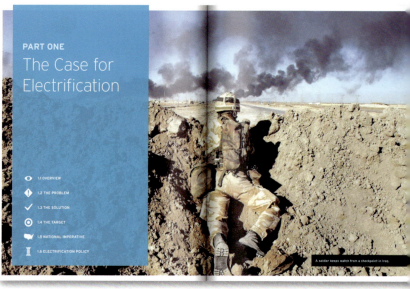

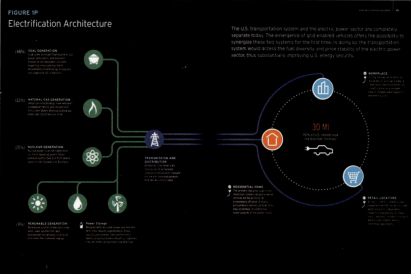

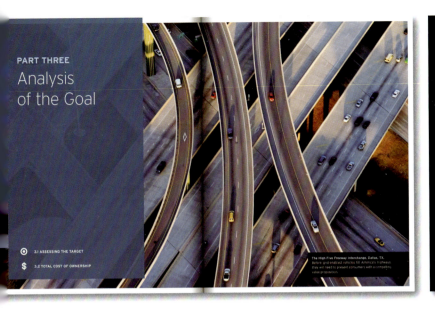

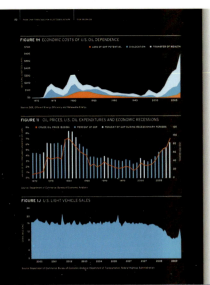

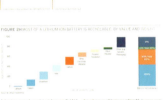

MetroSouth Medical Center

After rescuing a 103-year hospital in Chicago's south suburbs from closing, newly named MetroSouth Medical Center needed to quickly begin building a trusted brand capable of continuing and growing long-standing relationships. No stone could be left unturned in transforming the brand on-site and in the community.

With a focus on creating superior patient and practitioner experiences, MetroSouth's vision is translated to every aspect of the hospital's brand. A comprehensive strategy reaches out to patients, physicians, employees, volunteers and the community at large with an inspiring commitment to delivering the highest-quality healthcare experience in every way.

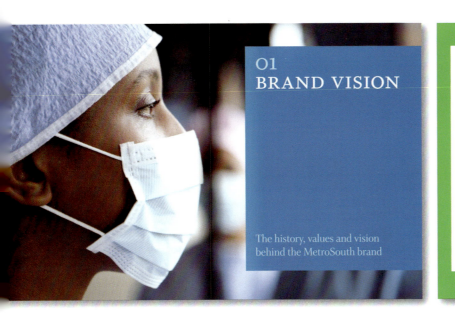

**01
BRAND VISION**

The history, values and vision
behind the MetroSouth brand

Our Brand Values

+ **Creating exceptional health care experiences** is the single greatest responsibility we have to our patients and practitioners.

+ **Being mindful of the needs of physicians and nurses** helps them provide the best quality care and creates the best environment in which to do it.

+ **Access to high-quality health care** means more than making sure it is easy to receive—it is also ensuring that patients feel welcome and are made a priority while they are here.

+ **MetroSouth is a family** that takes time to laugh, listen and learn; we make patients part of our family by extending to them the same appreciation we share for one another.

+ **Our diversity is our strength** and each of us is enriched by the different cultures, backgrounds and personal beliefs of our patients and fellow practitioners.

When employees, physicians and medical professionals experience the MetroSouth brand, we want them to see us as being…

+ **A family-like environment** that is a great place to work.

+ **A successful, growing hospital** that combines financial strength with agility and flexibility.

+ **A proactive culture** that encourages employee participation and recognizes individual contributions and achievement.

+ Highly **respectful and mindful of their business priorities**; responsive to their needs and the issues they face.

+ **A sustainable business** that knows its market thoroughly, and which has highly optimized internal operations.

+ Synonymous with the highest degree of professional **medical excellence**.

Touch Foundation

Founded and led by a McKinsey & Company director, Touch Foundation is leading the way to create sustainable change Tanzania's healthcare infrastructure. The non-profit organization sought to differentiate their brand and communicate the results-driven approach born of their McKinsey heritage.

A new brand identity is built on crisp typography and classic colours, while a re-structured website communicates Touch Foundation's business model, showcases results and shares knowledge resources. Special event design extends the core brand in refreshing ways to create a cohesive look that's right at home in any venue.

More Frontline Healthcare Workers

Interventions in the Healthcare System

CREATING PUBLIC AND PRIVATE PARTNERSHIPS
TO DELIVER EFFECTIVE SOLUTIONS

The Touch Foundation understands that it is not enough to
train new healthcare workers if the health system in which
they work is not significantly strengthened. The supply of
medicines to rural areas, referral to district hospitals and
better preventive care are critical.

*The Touch Foundation has taken a
pragmatic and analytical approach
to systems development to understand how to best improve health
in Tanzania and, by extension,
in other countries. By creating a
partnership in the Lake Zone that
brings together complementary
skills and the required resources, the
Touch Foundation has actually been
able to accomplish more through
those partnerships than the partners
could do on their own. They offer
business acumen, technical know-
how and the strong respect of the
Tanzanian government. Few organizations bring this combination
of assets to the table.*

JEFFREY STURCHIO
President and CEO, Global Health Council

Interventions in the Healthcare System

A Presidential Call to Action
Tanzania's President calls on political and business
leaders to support the Touch Foundation

Events in London and New York highlight the
growing momentum behind the Touch Foundation's
plan to develop public-private partnerships to
improve healthcare delivery in Tanzania.

The Touch Foundation and Barrick Gold hosted
a dinner honoring President Jakaya M. Kikwete
of Tanzania. President Kikwete remarked: "I
came here to ask all of you to continue to assist
the Touch Foundation. Build the capacity so that
they can help us ... train the doctors who are go-
ing to save so many lives — the women who are
in need, the children who are dying of malaria,
the many people who are dying of diseases that
can be cured, diseases that can be eliminated."

The theme of the evening was the necessity for
partnership across public and private sectors
to achieve wider access to healthcare in Africa,
especially in Tanzania. Touch Foundation
President Lowell Bryan noted that President
Kikwete is demonstrating great leadership in

Tanzania by prioritizing improved access to
healthcare — including in the most rural areas.

Those who joined the President at the event
included: Ambassador Goosby, U.S. Global
AIDS Coordinator, Professor Mwakyusa,
Tanzania's Minister of Health and Social
Welfare, Ambassador Mahiga, Permanent
Representative of Tanzania to the UN;
Ambassador Sefue, Tanzanian Ambassador to
the U.S.; and Ambassadors Green and Parham,
formerly U.S. Ambassador and U.K. High
Commissioner to Tanzania, respectively.

The subsequent Touch Foundation event
in London, hosted by the Tanzanian High
Commissioner, drew together corporate and
public sector leaders. This event marked
the first in a series of events to mobilize the
Tanzanian and business communities in the
United Kingdom.

TouchFoundation

BARRICK

◄ Dock workers on Lake Victoria

Achieving Better Health 23

*The university has come a long way
since we started the M.D. program in
2003. The growth in the number of M.D.
students as well as students in other
health cadres has been dramatic. While
we still have a long road ahead, I am
encouraged that fewer Tanzanians will
die needlessly from the major killers that
are preventable and treatable, thanks
to the increasing output of committed
Bugando graduates.*

PROFESSOR JACOB MTABAJI
Principal, Bugando University
College of Health Sciences

Bugando Graduate Blazes Trail:
An Interview with Stella Mongella
from the First M.D. Class

Why did you choose medicine?

I wanted to give back to my country. Tanzania
faces a great deficit in healthcare professionals,
and I hope to play my small part by being the
best doctor I can be. I hope to be able to provide
much needed, quality healthcare to the many
disadvantaged people.

What do you enjoy the most about being a doctor?

I enjoy the day-to-day contact with patients —
admitting a patient who is very ill, doing investiga-
tions and coming up with a diagnosis, and actually
helping the patient get better at the end of the day.
It's a good feeling when you're able to help someone
to return to her daily activities, especially when you
know that this is a mother of five children and she
has a home to take care of.

**What did the Touch Foundation's scholarship
mean to you?**

It has meant the possibility of becoming a
doctor! I come from a family of civil servants
and really can't afford the 20 million Tanzanian
Shillings.* I'm not alone in the family — I have

my younger siblings — so everyone has to go to
school. The scholarship has meant a lot because
it actually enabled me to pursue and complete
my medical education.

Have you faced additional challenges?

At the end of the day, one of the biggest challenges that comes with being a female doctor is
having to work your hardest so as to prove that
you are as good as your male counterparts in all
aspects of clinical work.

**What have you been up to since completing
medical school?**

I finished a one-year internship at Bugando
Medical Centre and I am now in my first year
of Bugando's Masters in Medicine program.
Ultimately, I want to be a pediatrician.

*To watch an interview that
the PBS "NewsHour" with
Jim Lehrer" conducted
with Stella, visit the "Films"
section of our website,
www.touchfoundation.org,
under "News & Resources."

* This is approximately $35,000 for tuition alone. By
comparison, a medical student in the United States pays
an average of $124,000 for his or her medical education.

Achieving Better Health 25

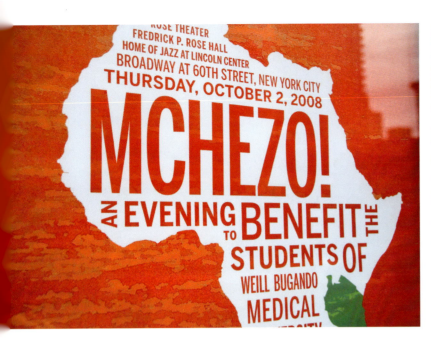

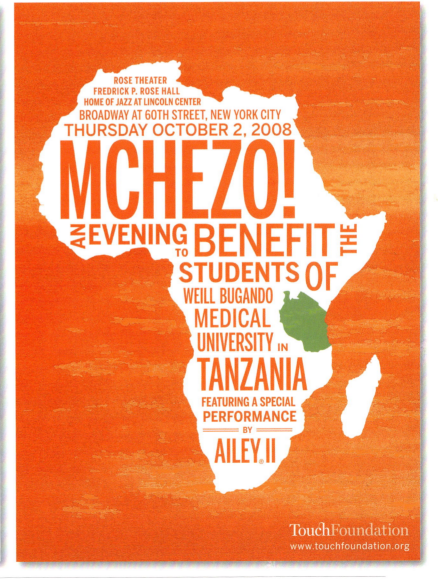

Proclivity

How does one put a human face on a predictive behavioral targeting engine that provides marketers with actionable sales intelligence? Proclivity Systems sought to communicate the promise of complex software to a non-technical audience.

Starting with a dynamic logo representing "data transformed", cross-media design extensions support sales and marketing initiatives — in person, online, and on the tradeshow floor. A restructured, optimized and redesigned application interface has improved Proclivity's software, empowering market traders to control incredibly powerful data with ease.

Black Umbrella

Black Umbrella builds practical, efficient disaster plans for individuals, couples and families. The client chose the name umbrella for its symbolism of protection. MyORB wanted to build upon this idea in the branding design. As most of their services are for an individuals' or families' home, the designers used the outer shape of an umbrella as a shield for the house. The logo can be used on its own or can be combined with a complex grid which represents the intricate network of connections and services.

Creative Director: Lucie Kim
Designers: Lucie Kim, Felix von der Weppen

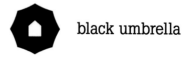

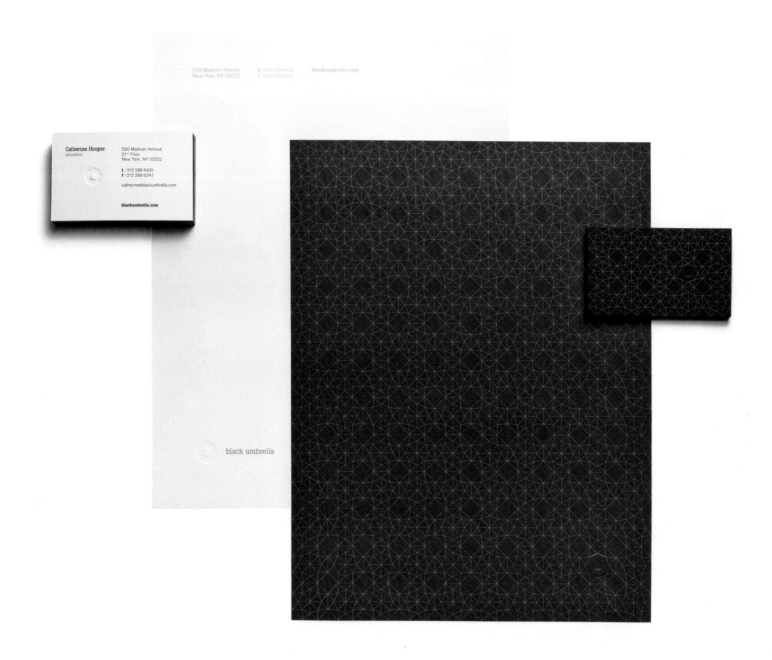

Tramelan

onlab created the new corporate identity and visual language for the town of Tramelan in Switzerland between 2004 and 2008, later translating the concept into various extensive media and applications.

As an urgent response to 25 years of economic regression in Tramelan, an interdisciplinary commission was assigned with the task of examining the identity and development opportunities of the town. onlab was invited to contribute as advisors in the field of communication. After the final report, onlab was commissioned to develop a new visual identity and communication strategy for the town in 2006 and for the years to come.

Key terms of the communication strategy derived from the cultural and historic traits of Tramelan were identified as "Savoir Faire" representing the know-how and craftsmanship of the watchmaker industry and the "Savoir Vivre" representing the authentic lifestyle of the population. These key terms served as the conceptual framework for colour-coding as well as other formal design features of the visual identity.

onlab took inspiration from the local industrial tradition and watchmaking culture in the design for the exclusive typeface "Tramelan-Lutz". The new emblem and logo are based on this newly created typeface. This approach provided a strong uniformity and clarity for all the media.

AJKRYÉÀÔ→

Lutz, Cornel Windlin, Lineto, 2002

AJKRYÉÀÔ→

Tramelan-Lutz, Mika Mischler, onlab, 2007

Operation Butterfly

Saalburg Roman Fort

The Saalburg Roman Fort is the world's only recon-structed Roman fort and archaeological museum – just next to the Limes World Heritage site, the ancient frontier between the Roman Empire and the Germanic tribal territories.

Operation Butterfly is responsible for the clear line in their offline communication.

Creative direction & design: Balázs Tarsoly

David Ari Leon is an award-winning, Emmy-nominated composer/music supervisor who has worked for studios including Fox, ABC, NBC, Marvel and Lionsgate, and has six successful CDs under his belt. EDG produced this progressive mark that reflects David's passion for music and the arts. His brand identity includes an animated web page bio, where his logo comes alive with synchronized music scored by David with Flash animation created by EDG (www.soundmindmusic.net). David could not be more thrilled with what he termed "such an entertaining and effective solution." This design strategy provides a core business asset for David, ensuring that his self-promotion stays at the same high level as his extraordinary musical talent.

Designers: Dallas Duncan, Mark Sojka
Art Director: Stan Evenson

GGI Office

GGI has been delivering quality workplace solutions to some of Australia's leading businesses since 1996 and remains focused on developing lasting relationships with all of its clients, large and small. GGI delivers the clean lines, exceptional customisation and ergonomic essentials that contemporary offices demand - regardless of how limited they are by space or budget.

GGI needed a brand update to clearly communicate its position at the top-end of the office furniture middle market. The new look and feel needed to capture GGI's core values and brand personality and differentiate the company from its competitors.

PDC Creative looked to its understanding of the target market to create a premium but friendly brand identity and brand personality for GGI. The range of customers – from corporates to architects and designers – meant the look and feel needed to be contemporary, appealing to the design community and convey a professional aesthetic appropriate for the corporate market.

With the tagline, "Make Space Work", PDC Creative developed the brand identity, communication and website expressing the brand through a combination of visual language and tone of voice.

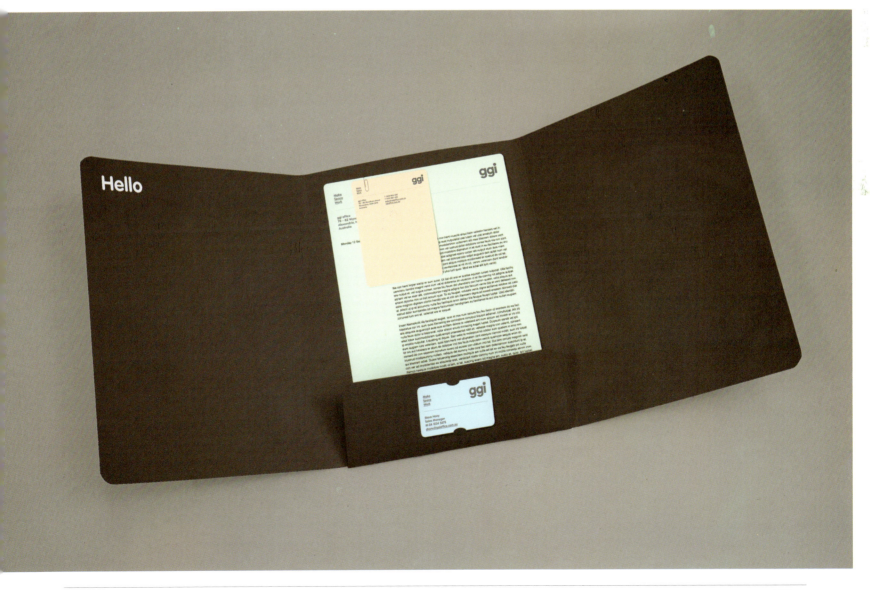

Grosvenor Place

Grosvenor Place, with its tower building conceived by renowned international architect Harry Seidler, occupies an entire Sydney city block and is home to more than 5,000 employees from the world's leading companies. It is one of a small number of premium grade commercial buildings in Sydney.

Despite its independent assessment as a premium grade commercial building, the market perception of Grosvenor Place was lagging far behind the quality of the offer. Grosvenor Place urgently needed to update its brand positioning to stave off significant impending vacancies.

Through a holistic, integrated identity program, PDC Creative reengineered the brand to represent its premium qualities and ensure consistency across all branded collateral. To follow, PDC Creative designed a targeted marketing campaign that addressed different segments of the market and delivered relevant and compelling communication to each.

Newspaper and magazine advertising, print collateral, signage, interactive EDMs, a website and several targeted DM campaigns made up the new approach.

The whole campaign culminated in a limited edition coffee table book, Icon — Grosvenor Place, Biography of a Building.

The clients were highly impressed with PDC:

"PDC Creative have provided the highest quality work positioning our brand in a very competitive market. I have been impressed with their professionalism and their ability to deliver innovative and truly workable solutions. Their understanding of our objectives and response to our needs has proved invaluable."

PDC Creative

Sensory Journeys

PDC Creative conceived a new revenue-generating proposition for Moët Hennessy Australia (MHA). Based on events, called Sensory Journeys, guests would receive a truly luxurious and memorable brand experience – while forging an emotional and sustainable connection with the brand and thus becoming powerful brand ambassadors.

PDC Creative was charged with communicating this entirely new proposition both internally and to a niche target market.
In line with MHA's strategic business imperatives, brand leadership and the creation of exciting consumer and trade experiences were pivotal to this project.

PDC Creative developed an independent brand identity for Sensory Journeys, accompanied by a luxurious brochure containing comprehensive information for prospective customers.
A website outlining the brand messages and the innovative characteristics of the program was also developed by PDC Creative.

STEVE TODHUNTER

0400 669 288

steve.todhunter@moet-hennessy.com.au
www.sensoryjourneys.com

www.sensoryjourneys.com

Gingerbread Folk

PDC Creative refreshed the brand identity of Gingerbread Folk to secure its position at the premium end of the market, and to launch its new, sustainable and biodegradable packaging. Gingerbread Folk required a distinctive, unified approach to its packaging that would cut through the cluttered retail environment and convey the personality and unique premium positioning of the brand. The packaging also had to reflect the company's core principles as an environmentally responsible manufacturer using all-natural ingredients to produce high-end products.

PDC Creative tapped into the brand's distinctive style and quality of icing decoration to bring a premium but friendly brand identity and brand personality to Gingerbread Folk.

The essence of Gingerbread Folk is a wholesome, natural choice with a conscious, sustainable approach to environmental questions for both product and packaging.

PDC Creative developed the brand identity and packaging for the entire range as well as collateral covering the brand philosophy, product ingredients and environmentally sustainable packaging materials.

The sense of fun, combined with a certain level of sophistication, is designed to capture the hearts and minds of consumers.

Popcorn Design / Ross Gunter

Weber Shandwick Invite

Invitation design for Weber Shandwick's 10th anniversary party held at the Saatchi Gallery in London. The designers wanted to produce something special and contemporary to mark the occasion. They designed invitations that on the front side carried a custom-designed, foiled "10" printed on Pristine White Colorplan, and were backed with Ebony Colorplan with foiled text. Posted in matching Ebony envelopes. Printed by Generation Press.

popcornbox.com / rossgunter.com / webershandwick.co.uk / generationpress.co.uk

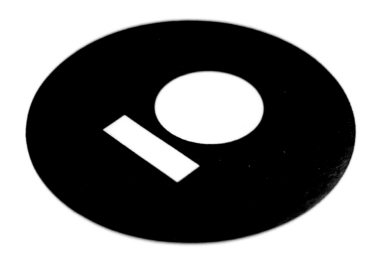

Thursday 20th January 2011
7pm–10pm
Saatchi Gallery, Duke of York's
King's Road, London, SW3 4RY
—
RSVP to Nicola Pallett
npallett@webershandwick.com
+44 (0) 20 7067 0899

Strictly by invitation only
(Invitations are non-transferable)

Copenhagen Parts

How do you create a small independent bicycle brand for bicycle connoisseurs without being too commercial or too deliberately underground?

The name is of course taken from the name of the origin city, Copenhagen, and the fact that people talk about "Copenhagenizing" a city to refer to making a city bike-friendly.

The Copenhagen Parts identity designed by Mads Jakob Poulsen is clean, quirky and red! The logo is a reference to the way people find different parts and put them together to create their perfect bike/companion, graphically represented in a way that is unusual and un-commercial for its strategy of "deconstructing" the name. This nonetheless catches the eye and makes for a memorable identity.

Made at Goodmorning Technology / www.gmtn.dk

Weiss Contractors

Weiss Contractors is a Dallas-based commercial construction company that specializes in corporate interiors and commercial building construction. Range helped Weiss Contractors elevate their image and awareness through the development of smart and functional capabilities brochures that reflected their commitment to quality services.

Designer: John Swieter
Creative Director: John Swieter
Photographer: Karl Ludwig
Writer: Mogen Kuriyakin

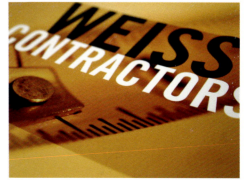

Predium

Predium is a commercial real estate firm that required an identity program that distinguished it from other competitors. They needed a name, a brand and a vocabulary that reflected a higher level of service and thinking. Range created a comprehensive identity program that gave Predium the building blocks to help the company grow.

Designer: John Swieter, Ray Gallegos
Creative Director: John Swieter
Illustrator: Ray Gallegos
Writer: Wayne Geyer

The building that DesignInsight acquired for their new showroom was in a state of advanced disrepair. On the second floor, amid bricks, dust and peeling wallpaper was an aquarium. And in that aquarium a goldfish was alive and well. Operation Butterfly's concept for reflecting DesignInsight's modern interiors with ageless style and ever-lasting quality was the idea of "contemporary antiques" which soon led to the goldfish becoming the logo. The corporate design developed from there.

Creative direction & design: Balázs Tarsoly

Roycroft Design

Protiam

To go from a startup business to a successful concern, this software company needed a logo, identity and website to help it stand out. Roycroft Design delivered the complete package.

After winning "Best of Show" at an important paper trade fair, Mohawk Paper commissioned Roycroft Design to create a piece promoting the printability of their 50/10 paper. Another award-winning job.

Roycroft Design

Expect Miracles

Roycroft Design crafted this invitation for Mutual Funds Against Cancer and helped make this wine-tasting fundraiser the toast of the town.

Bette Troy

Elegance, personality, and attention to detail describe the work of photo stylist Bette Troy. Roycroft Design kept these elements in mind when crafting her logo, business card and stationery.

Sawdust

CloserStill

A logo mark and identity projecting growth and
prosperity — qualities that CloserStill bring to
the companies they invest in.

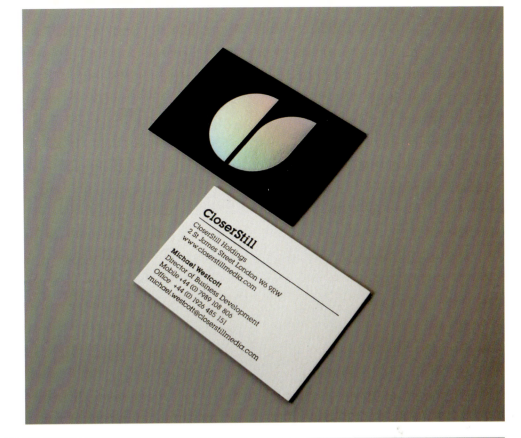

Sign*

Tenbosch House

Tenbosch House is characterized by its corporate philosophy of caring discreetly. In a typical Brussels Art Nouveau townhouse furnished with a carefully chosen selection of mid 20th Century Scandinavian furniture, the owners have conceived 7 bright suites, with terraces and balconies.

Sign* designed the comprehensive house style and the website – both of which are elegant and classical with a touch of modernity.

Creative Director: Franck Sarfati
Designer: Astrid Verdeyen

Eddy Merckx Cycles

Eddy Merckx, the famous cycling champion, started his small factory in 1980. Over a period of almost 30 years, this small company has developed and commercialised high-end bicycles, both in Belgium and abroad.

The new owner of the company has put in place a business development plan with the ambition to sell a substantially larger number of bicycles per year within a period of 3-4 years. A wider range of bikes is being developed, including medium range products, with prices starting at a more accessible level.

To achieve this goal, the company required a strong brand image that could help them reposition themselves in the market; an image that would be credible, attractive and convincing for a wide spectrum of customers, from the USA to Japan.

The new brand identity developed by Sign* for Eddy Merckx Cycles is anchored in the personality of its legendary founder, Eddy Merckx himself. The new logo is contemporary, dynamic and expresses velocity through its typography. In addition, it conveys the fighting spirit through the aggressive shape of the symbol that represents the M of Merckx, while also containing references to the V of victory, steep mountains, the teeth of a cannibal (in reference to Merckx's nickname on the racing circuit), and the folded form of old-style handlebars.

Creative Director: Franck Sarfati
Designer: Cédric Aubrion
Copywriter: Gavin Watt

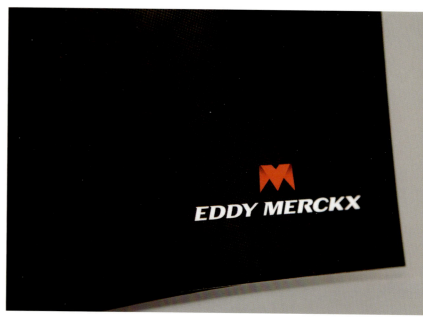

EDDY HAS ALWAYS BEEN OBSESSED WITH BIKES.

In fact it wasn't unusual for him to get up in the middle of the night to change something on his handlebars or gears. Position, fit and feel are incredibly important for him - on his own bike and on those of others too. This innate understanding of how a bike should be - a result of talent and many years of experience - is key for the design of every Eddy Merckx bicycle.

It is a true story that Eddy took a bike apart to find out how many parts it comprised. **THE ANSWER?** 1,125 separate pieces. "I must have been mad".

Fingerprint Business Cards

An identity for a company whose approach to marketing is 'individualized', i.e. they use a scientific method to reach their target audience (NEOs). Fingerprint Strategies challenges the status quo in a no-bullshit fashion by taking an approach to sales that has not been seen in the market today.

Creative Director: Rob Schlyecher
Designer: Perry Chua
Art Director: James Filbry
Copywriter: Rob Schlyecher

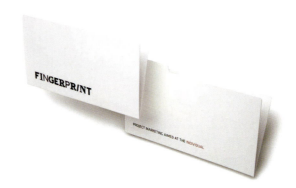

The concept behind the design of these business cards was to engage, innovate and repurpose. Contact details were printed on stickers that were then adhered to a variety of different laminate samples to underline the importance of functionality, individuality and custom design.

Creative Director: Perry Chua
Designer: Perry Chua
Art Director: Perry Chua

Select Wines Business Cards

The client commissioned Spring Advertising to redesign their logo to communicate a strong focus on quality with a design that appealed to the senses, like their wines. The new strategy strengthened the 'Select' component of the brand name in relation to 'Wines'. Employees' names appear in their own handwriting on the front, and real cork was used on the back of the business cards.

Creative Director: Rob Schlyecher
Designer: Perry Chua
Art Director: James Filbry
Copywriter: Rob Schlyecher

Thomas Billingsley Business Cards

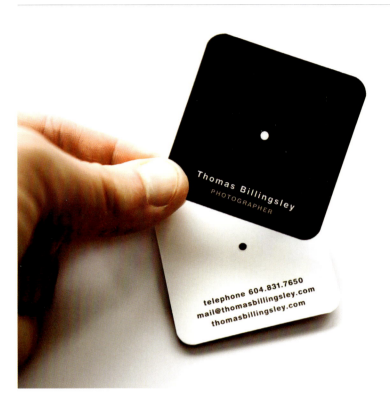

The client, Thomas Billingsley, gave Spring Advertising a brief that included this important statement, "My work is precise and it pulls you in to take a second look". To demonstrate the precision of his work, we designed the stationery so that the circular hold lined up perfectly with the crosshair every time you inserted the card into the sleeve.

Creative Director: Perry Chua
Designer: Perry Chua
Art Director: Perry Chua

Talk 1410 Business Cards

The Talk 1410 stationery was developed to reflect the talk radio station's branding statement, "Be Quotable". The perforated business card is an instant guerilla-advertising tool for users to create their own quotable content.

Creative Director: Rob Schlyecher
Designer: Perry Chua
Art Director: James Filbry
Copywriter: Rob Schlyecher

Another fruitful harvest! That's the response received time and again from satisfied customers after entrusting the cultivation of their brand to Blake Brand Growers (BBG). Once you peel back that shiny exterior skin, it's that succulent, juicy in-depth analysis and creative flow that BBG delivers for products, services and companies, year after fruitful year. With that said, how would you brand a branding expert? Working closely with BBG's founder and proprietor, Jeff Blake, Evenson Design Group was able to deliver an orchard full of organic ideas. As you can see by the appropriate and wildly nostalgic orange crate imagery, the new brand identity plants the seeds to keep Blake Brand Growers ripe with success.

Designers: Katja Loesch, Mark Sojka
Illustrator: Wayne Watford
Art Director: Stan Evenson

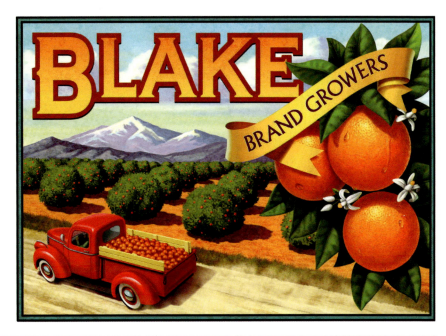

Spunk Design Machine

Davis Food Co-op

The Davis Food Co-op, one of the largest natural food co-ops in California, faced an influx of competition from two new chain stores opening in the city of Davis. In order to help Davis Food Co-op fortify its stake as an indispensable piece of the city, Spunk updated the co-op's brand to reflect a local, progressive, and welcoming institution.

As part of the brand update, Spunk developed the simple, but powerful message "Welcome to Davis." This message reinforces that Davis Food Co-op is a place where all community members are welcome and helps dispel the stereotype that it's just a "hippie" hangout. Additionally, "Welcome to Davis" invites the people of Davis and surrounding communities to view Davis Food Co-op as an icon of the city — something the chain stores will never be. All of Spunk's work on the Davis Food Co-op honors its history, construction, and location in a major agricultural center, all the while invigorating the brand look and feel to propel the co-op to a successful future.

Creative Director, Art Director: Jeff Johnson
Senior Designer, Writer: Steve Marth
Illustrator: Lucas Richards, Steve Marth

THOUSAND HILLS FARMS
97% Lean Ground Beef

$7.99/lb.

THOUSAND HILLS FARMS
97% Lean Ground Beef

$7.99/lb.

THOUSAND HILLS FARMS
97% Lean Ground Beef

$7.99/lb.

THOUSAND HILLS FARMS
97% Lean Ground Beef

$7.99/lb.

BASKET ENVY?
DAVIS NOW OFFERS FREE USE OF **THE FLYING TOMATO** GROCERY GETTERS

Sign out a Burley, haul your groceries home, and just bring it back within 24 hours.

Having trouble attaching it to your bike? Ask one of our employees, and they'll gladly help you out.

THE FLYING TOMATO
GROCERY GETTER

WELCOME TO DAVIS
THEY SAY OUR CITY SPROUTED UP AROUND A RAILROAD DEPOT IN 1868. **WE'D LIKE TO THINK IT HAPPENED ORGANICALLY.**

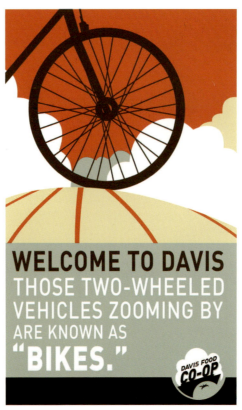

WELCOME TO DAVIS
THOSE TWO-WHEELED VEHICLES ZOOMING BY ARE KNOWN AS **"BIKES."**

WELCOME TO DAVIS
THANKFULLY, PLANS FOR THE **MAD DOG 20/20 CENTER** WERE VOTED DOWN.

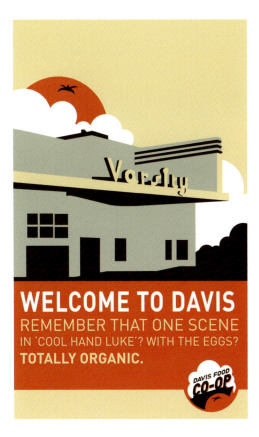

WELCOME TO DAVIS
REMEMBER THAT ONE SCENE IN 'COOL HAND LUKE'? WITH THE EGGS? **TOTALLY ORGANIC.**

DAVIS FOOD CO-OP

WELCOME TO DAVIS
JOIN OUR PETITION TO FILL THE WATER TOWER WITH **VANILLA SOY CHAI.**

DAVIS FOOD CO-OP

WELCOME TO DAVIS
PLEASE ENJOY OUR **RIDICULOUSLY LARGE TOMATO.**

DAVIS FOOD CO-OP

WELCOME TO DAVIS
BAGGIN' THE BAGGINS **SINCE NINETEEN SEVENTY-TWO**

DAVIS FOOD CO-OP

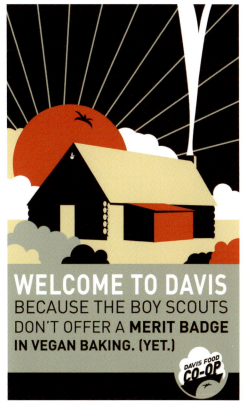

WELCOME TO DAVIS
BECAUSE THE BOY SCOUTS DON'T OFFER A **MERIT BADGE** IN VEGAN BAKING. (YET.)

DAVIS FOOD CO-OP

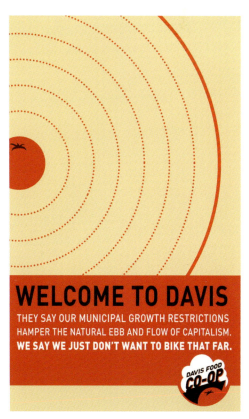

WELCOME TO DAVIS
THEY SAY OUR MUNICIPAL GROWTH RESTRICTIONS HAMPER THE NATURAL EBB AND FLOW OF CAPITALISM. **WE SAY WE JUST DON'T WANT TO BIKE THAT FAR.**

DAVIS FOOD CO-OP

Spunk Design Machine

Tank Goodness Cookies

Taste these hot-n-bothered gooey gourmet, let-the-chips-fall-where-they-may, delivered-to-your-door cookies, and flowers will wilt in comparison. Spunk mixed up the logo, package, website, stationery, T-shirts, promotional video and cookie car design: baking a brand that appeals to an audience hungry for sophisticated quality. Tank Goodness has grown from Anne and Dennis Tank's original home kitchen bakery to having licensed partners in five states. Rather than grow through the expensive franchise model, the Tanks have created a new low-cost licensing platform that stays true to their sustainable growth business values. They have never advertised and continue to grow their business by delivering one great cookie at a time.

Creative Director: Jeff Johnson
Writer: Phil Calvit, Ben Pagel
Designers: Steve Jockisch, Jason Walzer
Illustrators: Steve Jockisch, Jason Walzer

Spunk had the privilege to design the new identity system for The University of Minnesota College of Design, which includes everything from logos and style guides to websites and motion graphics. The College of Design has an identity that focuses on humanity and curiosity. These attributes are encapsulated in the simple question form "What If...?" and the transformative process of the design is fulfilled through the application of photography, patterns, color bars and the transforming "M".

Creative Director/Art Director: Jeff Johnson
Senior Designers: Andrew Voss, Steve Marth
Writer: Ben Pagel

Square Feet Design

208 West 96

208 West 96 is a boutique condominium comprised of nine full-story residences. Set in Manhattan's iconic Upper West Side, this contemporary new development constitutes a stylish addition to this storybook neighborhood. Square Feet Design played off the "full-storied" theme, creating a narrative inspired by the structure of a novel. Aesthetically, they created an overlapping graphic motif of mesh patterns similar to the metal mesh of the balconies on the façade of the building. The campaign's modern vibe evoked the building's downtown loft-like architectural style.

Creative Director: Lauren Marwil
Designers: Marcella Kovac, Robyn Cooperstein
Renderer: Kim Wendell Design
Writer: Erin Newton
Client: Manor Properties Group LLC

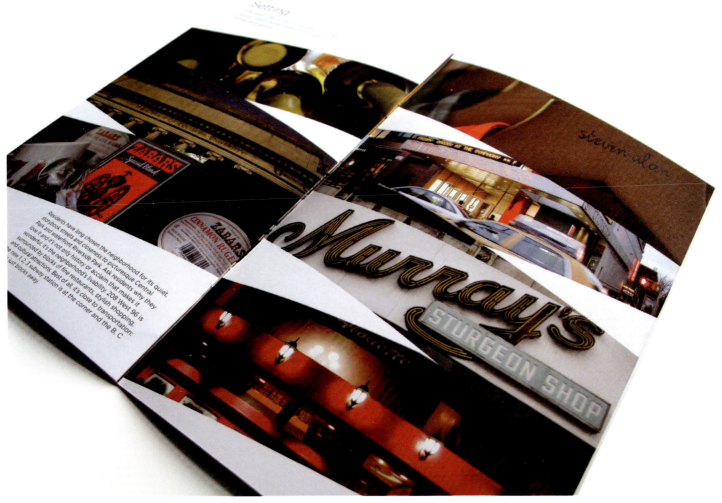

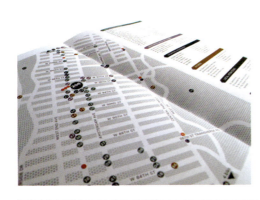

Square Feet Design

930 Poydras

Square Feet Design developed a campaign for 930 Poydras, a 250-unit high-rise that challenged prospective tenants to "Rethink Vertical Living." The campaign centered on highlighting the building's extensive list of amenities and their 9th floor "sky-lobby" designed to give residents a community hub such as New Orleanians are accustomed to, while providing the ultimate experience in luxury rental living. The graphic style of the campaign was inspired by the metal and glass paneled façade that makes this building so unique in the New Orleans cityscape dominated by low-rise historic structures. The black and white patterns and panels gave the campaign a minimalist, modern feel.

Creative Director: Lauren Marwil
Designers: Marcella Kovac, Michelle Snyder, Robyn Cooperstein
Photographer: Jackson Hill
Renderer: CG Render Visualization Studio, Inc.
Writer: Erin Newton
Client: Brian Gibbs Development

Square Feet Design

Crescent Club

The Crescent Club development has brought resort-style apartment living to the New Orleans area. The task of Square Feet Design was to create a brand and publicity campaign that appealed to the young, busy, social renter who would appreciate all that the Crescent Club had to offer — from fitness centers and swimming pools to concierge services.

Creative Director: Lauren Marwil
Designers: Marcella Kovac, Michelle Snyder
Photographer: Jackson Hill
Renderer: Kim Wendell Design
Client: Domain Companies

The Preserve

This high-end residential building that is leading the renaissance of New Orleans' Mid-City neighborhood is built on the site of an iconic former hot-sauce factory. In the aftermath of hurricane Katrina, during the rebuilding of the city, New Orleans pride was stronger than ever. Our task in creating a brand for this development was to design elements and language that exemplified the local flavors and culture that New Orleanians love so much.

Creative Director: Lauren Marwil
Designers: Marcella Kovac, Michelle Snyder
Photographer: Jackson Hill
Renderer: Kim Wendell Design, Aniphase
Client: Domain Companies

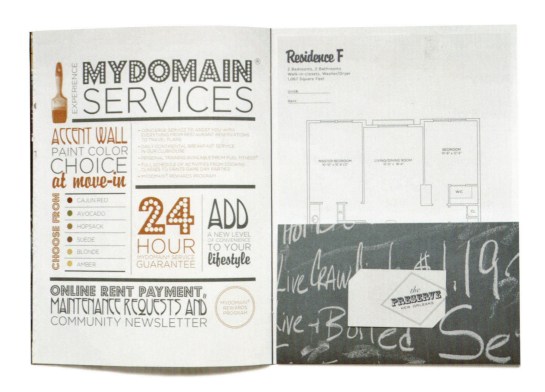

Anke Stohlmann Design

Maxwax

A boutique salon located on the Upper West Side of Manhattan specializing in body waxing, Maxwax prides itself on its ultra-clean environment, reasonable prices and exceptional service. Our design challenge was to create an identity that reflected the client's attention to detail and inherently human approach to their work. The look and feel we designed is clean, engaging and warm, and reflects the salon's comfortable surroundings and high-quality service. Capitalizing on the repetition of letters in the salon name, the logo contributes a playfulness to the identity that sets it apart from its competitors. In addition, Anke Stohlmann Design created the full line of packaging for Maxwax, including in-store menus, product labels, stationery and signage.

Eileen Margaret Cornell Principal
167 West 74 Street New York, NY 10023
Phone: 212.580.8040 Fax: 212.580.8047
mail@maxwaxnyc.com

maxwax® 167 West 74 Street New York, NY 10023

Studio Brave

Peter Rowland Catering

When Peter Rowland Catering first approached Studio Brave, they had a strong reputation but an outdated visual identity. Studio Brave updated the brand mark through an evolution and refreshed the entire colour palette and image library. Every piece of collateral was meticulously re-designed and protected by a brand guidelines document to ensure consistency.

Among the collateral is the tender which Peter Rowland submitted to the National Gallery of Victoria. They now provide the catering for the three cafés situated in the gallery.

Creative Director: Tim Sutherland
Designers: Adrian Colling, Alec Macfarlane

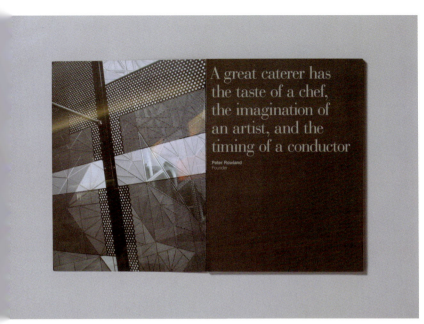

PETER ROWLAND

Southern Star
Docklands

PETER ROWLAND

Port Melbourne Yacht Club
Port Melbourne

PETER ROWLAND

Melbourne Museum
Carlton

PETER ROWLAND

Gardens House
Royal Botanic Gardens

PETER ROWLAND
catering & events

Private & Corporate Catering

Peter Rowland Catering
exemplifies superb food,
impeccable service
and superior design –
every event, every time.

PETER ROWLAND

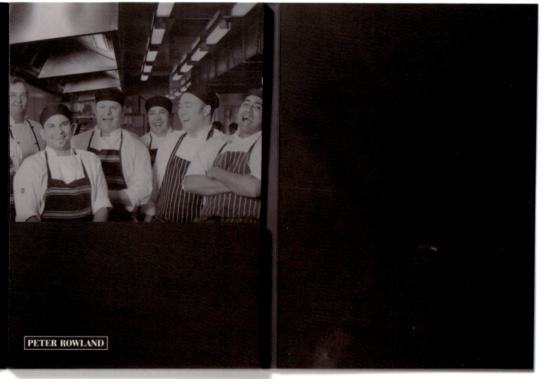

The Chapter House
Paul's Cathedral

The Ian Potter Centre: NGV Australia
Federation Square

NGV International
St Kilda Road

Rippon Lea
Elsternwick

Flemington - The Event Centre
Flemington

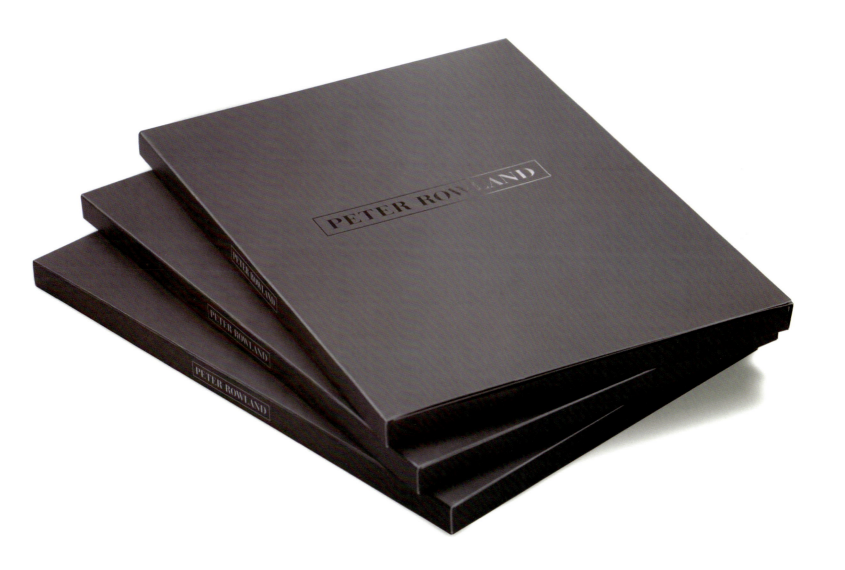

Tnop™ Design

Ruhaak

Ruhaak is Christina Ruhaak's textile and rug designs company. Based in Chicago, the company specializes in custom-designed rugs with a high level of hand detailing. The main challenge for the designers at Tnop™ Design was to create a logo and identity that would reflect Christina Ruhaak's design aesthetic and her thinking and working processes. The custom type on the logo came from the words "weave" and "thread" which represent textile and rug making. The logo represents Christina Ruhaak's design process. The colour scheme used in the identity was taken from one of Christina Ruhaak signature colour combinations.

Habitat® Promo Postcards

These are various promotional postcards for Habitat® furniture store in Bangkok. The postcards had to be designed and produced under a limited budget because they send out postcards throughout the year. The postcards are 5 × 7 in (127 X 178 mm) and employ unique printing techniques from 2-color printing, fluorescent color and foil stamping to embossing and liquid lamination.

Client: Habitat, Bangkok
Designers: Tnop Wangsillapakun, Akwit Vongsangiam, Wootinut Wangsillapakun

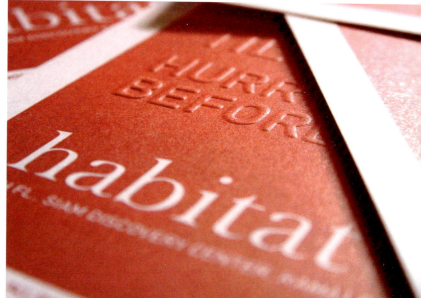

Undesign

Ilti Luce

Undesign had been working on the coordinated identity design project for Ilti Luce when they received some impressive news. The firm informed them that its brand had joined the Philips Group, the Dutch giant. It was official, they had signed the deal. The designers were particularly impressed and pleased that a company from their own city, with a particular regard for design, had made it: it had gone beyond national borders to conquer its own piece of the world.

Maxema

In the province of Turin in Italy, there is an area specialized in the production of ballpoint pens. This district started to build its reputation many years ago, thanks to the quality of the firms that were based there. One of these was Maxema. It started out as a small company but, thanks to its forward-looking approach, it soon became one of the most successful representatives of its sector abroad. When the designers from Undesign met the directors of Maxema, it was immediately evident to both parties that they were on the same wavelength. They shared the same sense of belonging to the Turin region and the same desire to go a long way. They parted with a mutual promise from each party to the other: "However far we get with our business we'll write you a post card. With a ballpoint pen, of course."

Softgarden

Development and execution of a complete corporate design solution for Softgarden GmbH, a company that develop eRecruiting software. The package included the design and delivery of stationery, product catalogues, and the company website as well as draughting white papers.

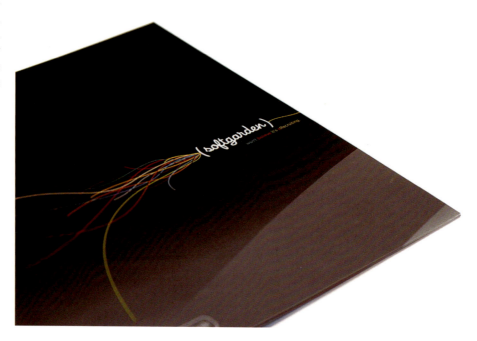

Invitation to the official opening of the Alicante Nespresso Boutique

The mailing consists of a red envelope with black stamped lettering and a black laminated invitation with red paper inside. The main characteristics of Nespresso's 16 coffee varieties are listed in 16 different gloss stampings which reflect the colours of the respective capsules.

St George's Day Nespresso Rose

Special St George's Day celebration pack offered in Nespresso Boutiques. A promotional element that simulates the traditional St George's Day gift of a rose. The piece created holds a Nespresso coffee capsule, that foms the head of the rose.

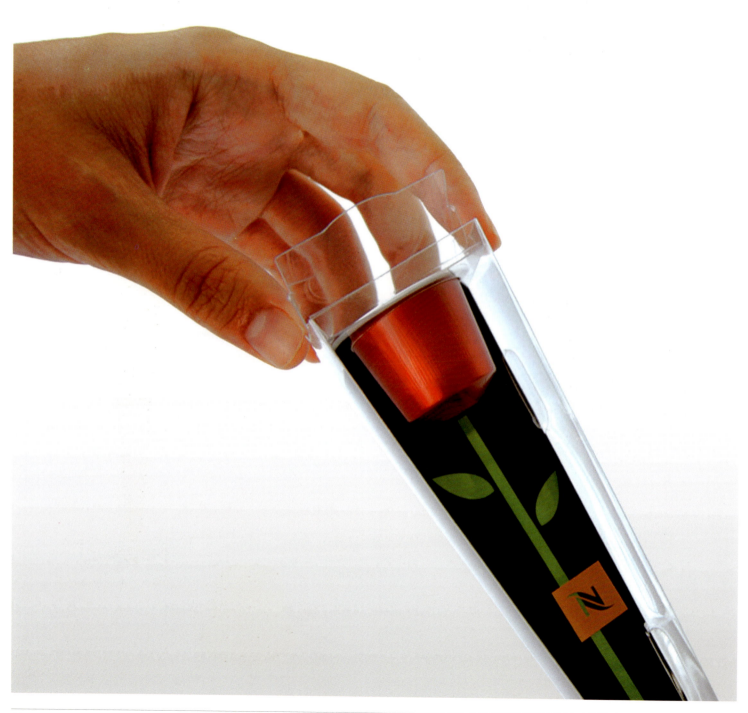

English Metas Identity

Naming and identity for English Metas. The brand naome is made from the following words: "English", the language and "Metas", (a pun on the Spanish word for a personal challenge and the initials of the core services the company provides – "Mentours, English Teaching And Services"). The self-adhesive stars, which form the basis of the new graphic identity for the brand, refer to the motivational method of awarding "good job stickers", used in American schools to reward students for their achievements.

mentours
english
teaching
& services

english metas

D66 Posters

A series of posters for the Amsterdam branch of the D66 political party, the liberal-democrats. The posters, which are distributed outside of the election period, emphasize the clarity of the party's viewpoints.

Each poster playfully tackles one topic or point of view, all within the strict rules of the D66 visual identity. The 'Gay, Yes' poster, was distributed at the time of the '2009 Gay Pride'. During the annual Amsterdam Cultural Night there was no escaping the 'Nightlife, Yes' message. Apart from the posters, the message was also spread with flyers. 'Studying, Yes' added a positive message at the start of the new academic year, while 2010 was heralded affirmatively with an exclamation mark!

IJsseldelta

IJsseldelta is the area surrounding the Dutch city of Kampen in the Netherlands. It is a strikingly beautiful area some 300 square kilometres in extension. The local authorities have the ambition of turning IJsseldelta into a major tourist attraction. In view of this, the regional tourist office and Nationaal Landschap IJsseldelta commssioned Matthijs van Leeuwen to develop the visual brand identity.

After a thorough positioning process which involved all stakeholders, G2K developed a visual identity that intends to reflect the area's connection with water through the use of the nautical alphabet of signalling flags.

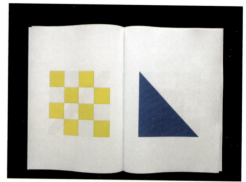

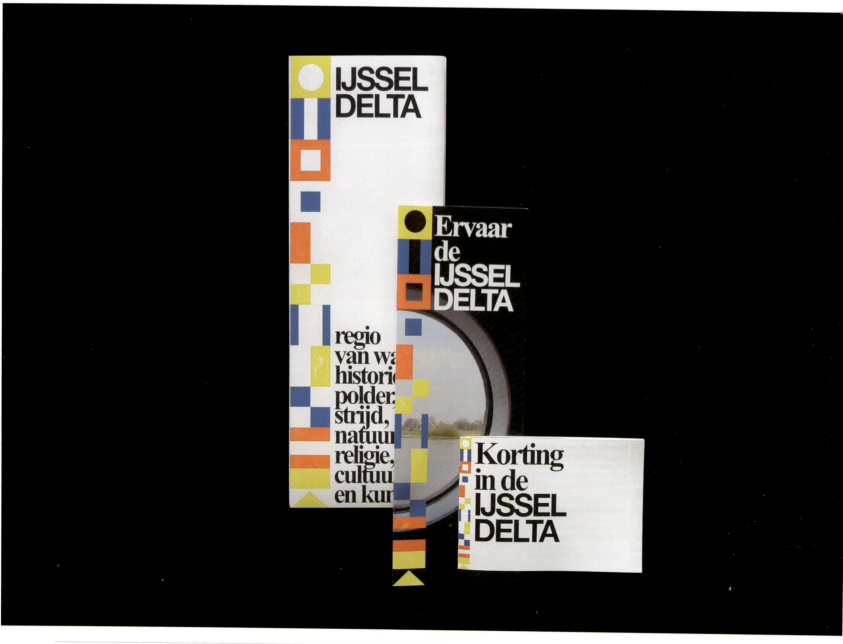

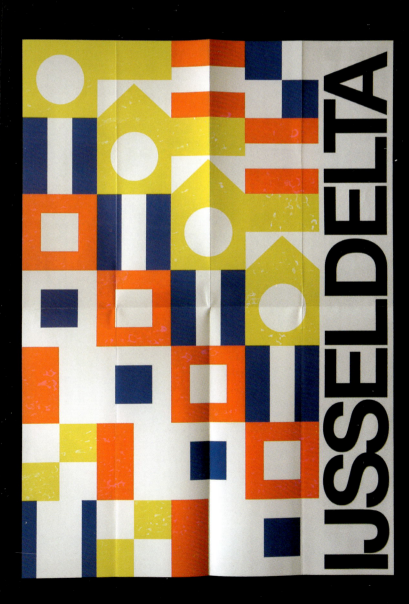

Designer Index

Anagrama

WEB:
www.anagrama.com
MAIL:
hello@anagrama.com
TEL:
+ 52 (81) 8336 6666
ADDRESS:
Francisco Naranjo 224, Colonia San Pedro,
66230, San Pedro Garza García, Nuevo León,
México
PAGES:
8-21

Anti

WEB:
www.anti-ink.com
MAIL:
kenneth@anti.as
TEL:
+(47) 934 45 238
ADDRESS:
Kristian Augustsgt. 13, 0164 Oslo, Norway
PAGES:
22-25

Asylum

WEB:
www.theasylum.com.sg
MAIL:
info@theasylum.com.sg
TEL:
+ 65 6324 2289
ADDRESS:
69 Circular Road, #03-01, Singapore, 049423
PAGES:
26-29

Atipus

WEB:
www.atipus.com
MAIL:
info@atipus.com
TEL:
+34 93 485 13 95
ADDRESS:
C/ Pallars 85, 1r 2a, 08018 Barcelona, Spain
PAGES:
30-31

Brogen Averill

WEB:
brogenaverill.com
MAIL:
brogen@thingwebsite.com
TEL:
+ 64 (0)21 277 2858
PAGES:
32-37

Believe in

WEB:
www.believein.co.uk
MAIL:
mail@believein.co.uk
TEL:
+ 44 (0) 1392 453000
ADDRESS:
33-35 Southernhay East, Exeter, EX1 1NX,
United Kingdom
PAGES:
38-49

Büro North

WEB:
www.buronorth.com
MAIL:
reception@buronorth.com
TEL:
+613 9654 3259
ADDRESS:
Level 1 / 35 Little Bourke Street
Melbourne, VIC 3000 Australia
PAGES:
50-51

Chen Design Associates

WEB:
www.chendesign.com
MAIL:
info@chendesign.com
TEL:
+1 415 896 5338
ADDRESS:
632 Commercial Street Fifth Floor
San Francisco, CA 94111-2599, USA
PAGES:
54

Chris Clarke

WEB:
www.chris-clarke.co.uk
MAIL:
mail@chris-clarke.co.uk
TEL:
+44 (0)7845 629 816
ADDRESS:
Unit 47, SODA studios
London, E8 4DG, UK
PAGES:
52-53

StudioConover

WEB:
www.studioconover.com
MAIL:
buildingcontexture@studioconover.com
TEL:
+1 619 238 1999
ADDRESS:
800 West Ivy Street, Studio C
San Diego, CA 92101, USA
PAGES:
55-57

COOEE

WEB:
cooee.nl
MAIL:
leon@cooee.nl
TEL:
+31 (0)6 183 972 97
ADDRESS:
Zuideinde 296
1035 PM Amsterdam, The Netherlands
PAGES:
58-61

Ina Cotsou

WEB:
www.inacotsou.com
MAIL:
mail@inacotsou.com
TEL:
+49 30 49 500 402
PAGES:
91

Counterform

WEB:
counterform.net
TEL:
+1 503 747 3765
ADDRESS:
10121 NW Fleetwood Drive
Portland, OR 97229, USA
PAGES:
62-67

Dalston Creative

WEB:
www.dalston.se
MAIL:
info@dalston.se
TEL:
+46 (0)76 028 20 51
ADDRESS:
Nybrogatan 34, 3tr, 114 39 Stockholm, Sweden
PAGES:
68-69

Detail

WEB:
www.detail.ie
MAIL:
mail@detail.ie
TEL:
+353 1 878 3168
ADDRESS:
11 The Friary, Bow Street, Smithfield,
Dublin 7, Ireland
PAGES:
70-73

Elixir Design

WEB:
www.elixirdesign.com
MAIL:
info@elixirdesign.com
TEL:
+ 1 415 834 0300
ADDRESS:
2134 Van Ness Avenue
San Francisco, CA 94102, USA
PAGES:
74-79

Calle Enstrom

WEB:
www.calleenstrom.se
MAIL:
calle@calleenstrom.se
PAGES:
80-81

espluga+associates

WEB:
www.espluga.net
MAIL:
info@espluga.net
TEL:
+34 93 362 10 51
ADDRESS:
Muntaner 269 1o 2a, 08021 Barcelona, Spain
PAGES:
82-85

Evenson Design Group

WEB:
www.evensondesign.com
MAIL:
sevenson@evensondesign.com
TEL:
+1 310 204 1995
ADDRESS:
4445 Overland Ave.
Culver City, CA 90230, USA
PAGES:
191, 223

Fridge Creative

WEB:
www.fridgecreative.co.uk
MAIL:
hello@fridgecreative.co.uk
TEL:
+44 (0) 20 7729 8661
ADDRESS:
59 Charlotte Road, Hoxton
London EC2A 3QT, United Kingdom
PAGES:
86-89

Golden Cosmos

WEB:
www.golden-cosmos.com
MAIL:
doris@golden-cosmos.com
PAGES:
90

Sebastian Gram

WEB:
www.sebastiangram.dk
MAIL:
sg@sebastiangram.dk
TEL:
+45 6022 8703
PAGES:
92-93

Hangar 18

WEB:
www.h18.com
MAIL:
info@h18.com
TEL:
+1 604 737 7111
ADDRESS:
Suite 220 1737 West 3rd Avenue
Vancouver BC Canada V6J 1K7
PAGES:
94-99

Hatch Design

WEB:
www.hatchsf.com
MAIL:
info@hatchsf.com
TEL:
+1 415 398 1650
ADDRESS:
402 Jackson Street
San Francisco, CA 94111, USA
PAGES:
100-101

Havnevik

WEB:
www.havnevik.no
MAIL:
mail@havnevik.no
TEL:
+47 70 11 56 00
ADDRESS:
Røysegt. 15, NO-6003 Ålesund, Norway
PAGES:
102-111

HI(NY)

WEB:
www.hinydesign.com
MAIL:
info@hinydesign.com
TEL:
+1 646 808 0708
ADDRESS:
401 Broadway Suite 1908
New York, NY 10013, USA
PAGES:
112-117

Hype & Slippers

WEB:
www.hypeandslippers.com
MAIL:
hello@hypeandslippers.com
TEL:
+44 (0) 117 325 1160
ADDRESS:
Bristol & Exeter House, Lower Approach Road,
Temple Meads, Bristol, BS1 6QS, UK
PAGES:
126-127

Hyperakt

WEB:
www.hyperakt.com
MAIL:
whatsup@hyperakt.com
TEL:
+1 718 855 4250
ADDRESS:
401 Smith Street, Brooklyn, NY, 11231, USA
PAGES:
118-125

ico Design

WEB:
www.icodesign.com
MAIL:
info@icodesign.com
TEL:
+44(0)20 7323 1088
ADDRESS:
75-77 Great Portland Street, London, W1W
7LR, United Kingdom
PAGES:
128-137

IlovarStritar

WEB:
www.ilovarstritar.com
MAIL:
info@ilovarstritar.com
TEL:
+386 41 751 363
ADDRESS:
Trdinova 5, Si-1000 Ljubljana, Slovenia
PAGES:
138-139

Lundgren+Lindqvist

WEB:
www.lundgrenlindqvist.se
MAIL:
hello@lundgrenlindqvist.se
TEL:
+46 (0) 736 90 90 11
ADDRESS:
Karl Johansgatan 72
SE-414 55 Gothenburg, Sweden
PAGES:
140-141

Melgrafik

WEB:
www.melgrafik.de
MAIL:
mail@melgrafik.de
TEL:
+49 160 8468769
PAGES:
142-143

Mind Design

WEB:
www.minddesign.co.uk
MAIL:
info@minddesign.co.uk
TEL:
+44 (0)20 7254 2114
ADDRESS:
Unit 33A, Regents Studios
8 Andrews Road, London E8 4QN, United
Kingdom
PAGES:
144-157

Mission Design

WEB:
www.mission.no
MAIL:
hello@mission.no
ADDRESS:
Henrik Ibsen Gate 100
0230 Oslo, Norway
PAGES:
158-159

Modelhart Design

WEB:
www.modelhart.at
MAIL:
design@modelhart.at
TEL:
+43 6412 4679-0
ADDRESS:
Ing.-Ludwig-Pech-Str. 1 _ 5600 St. Johann / Pg.
Austria
PAGES:
160-163

Moving Brands

WEB:
www.movingbrands.com
MAIL:
info@movingbrands.com
TEL:
+44 (0) 20 7739 7700
PAGES:
164-167

MSDS

WEB:
www.ms-ds.com
TEL:
+1 212-925-6460
ADDRESS:
611 Broadway, Suite 430
New York, NY 10012, USA
PAGES:
168-185

MyORB

WEB:
www.myorangebox.com
MAIL:
hello@myorangebox.com
TEL:
+1 212 226 4216
ADDRESS:
241 Centre Street 4th floor, New York, NY
10013, USA
PAGES:
186-187

onlab

WEB:
www.onlab.ch
TEL:
+49 (0)30 80 61 58 80
ADDRESS:
Oderberger Straße 11
10435 Berlin, Germany
PAGES:
188-189

Operation Butterfly

WEB:
www.operationbutterfly.com
MAIL:
contact@operationbutterfly.com
TEL:
+49 69 27 13 99 63
ADDRESS:
Kaiserstraße 61 D-60329, Frankfurt am Main,
Germany
PAGES:
190

PDC Creative

WEB:
www.pdccreative.com
MAIL:
matthew @pdccreative.com
TEL:
+ 61 2 9922 4411
ADDRESS:
125 Blues Point Road
 McMahons Point NSW 2060, Australia
PAGES:
192-199

Popcorn Design

WEB:
folio.popcornbox.com
MAIL:
studio@popcornbox.com
TEL:
+44 (0)207 199 9290
ADDRESS:
7 Tilney Court, Old Street
London EC1V 9BQ, United Kingdom
PAGES:
200-201

Mads Jakob Poulsen

WEB:
www.madsjakobpoulsen.dk
MAIL:
hello@madsjakobpoulsen.dk
PAGES:
202-203

Range

WEB:
www.rangeus.com
TEL:
+1 214 744 0555
ADDRESS:
2257 Vantage Street
Dallas, Texas 75207, USA
PAGES:
204-207

Roycroft Design

WEB:
www.roycroftdesign.com
MAIL:
info@roycroftdesign.com
TEL:
+1 617 720 4506
ADDRESS:
184 High Street, Suite 501
Boston, MA 02110, USA
PAGES:
208-211

Sawdust

WEB:
www.madebysawdust.co.uk
MAIL:
studio@madebysawdust.co.uk
TEL:
+44 (0) 20 7739 9787
ADDRESS:
Unit 2.04, 12–18 Hoxton Street
London N1 6NG, United Kingdom
PAGES:
212-213

Sign*

WEB:
www.designbysign.com
MAIL:
info@designbysign.com
TEL:
+32 2 218 20 70
ADDRESS:
57, Rue Locquenghien
1000 Brussels, Belgium
PAGES:
214-217

Spring Advertising

WEB:
www.springadvertising.com
MAIL:
grow@springadvertising.com
TEL:
+1 604 683 0167
ADDRESS:
Unit 301, 1250 Homer Street, Vancouver BC,
V6B 1C6, Canada
PAGES:
218-222

Spunk Design Machine

WEB:
spkdm.com
MAIL:
info@spkdm.com
TEL:
+1 612 724 3444
ADDRESS:
4933 34th Ave S
Minneapolis MN 55417, USA
PAGES:
224-231

Square Feet Design

WEB:
www.squarefeetdesign.com
MAIL:
info@squarefeetdesign.com
TEL:
+1 646 237 2828
ADDRESS:
11 Park Place, Suite 1705
New York, NY 10007, USA
PAGES:
232-239

Anke Stohlmann Design

WEB:
www.ankestohlmanndesign.com
MAIL:
info@ankestohlmanndesign.com
TEL:
+1 646 808 0691
PAGES:
240-241

Studio Brave

WEB:
studiobrave.com.au
MAIL:
info@studiobrave.com.au
ADDRESS:
Level 5, 289 Flinders Lane
Melbourne VIC 3000, Australia
PAGES:
242-245

TNOP™ DESIGN

WEB:
tnop.com
MAIL:
info@tnop.com
TEL:
+1 312 235 0170
ADDRESS:
1440 S Michigan Ave #322
Chicago IL 60605-2956, USA
PAGES:
246-249

Undesign

WEB:
undesign.it
MAIL:
info@undesign.it
TEL:
+39 011 56 11 755
ADDRESS:
Via Saluzzo 42
10125, Torino, Italy
PAGES:
250-253

upstruct

WEB:
www.upstruct.com
MAIL:
mail@upstruct.com
TEL:
+49 30 702 207 78
ADDRESS:
Alexandrinenstraße 4, 10969, Berlin, Germany
PAGES:
254-255

UVE

WEB:
www.estudiouve.com
MAIL:
uve@estudiouve.com
TEL:
+34 934 870 870
ADDRESS:
Diputación 323, 1º 1ª, 08009, Barcelona, Spain
PAGES:
256-261

Matthijs van Leeuwen

WEB:
www.matthijsvanleeuwen.com
MAIL:
contact@matthijsvanleeuwen.com
TEL:
+1 862 371 6224
PAGES:
262-265